LEADING IMPROVEMENT IN
LITERACY TEACHING AND LEARNING

Published in 2025 by Amba Press, Melbourne, Australia
www.ambapress.com.au

First published in 2022 by ACER Press, an imprint of
Australian Council for Educational Research Ltd

© Robyn Cox 2022

This book is copyright. All rights reserved. Except under the
conditions described in the *Copyright Act 1968* of Australia and
subsequent amendments, and any exceptions permitted under
the current statutory licence scheme administered by Copyright
Agency (www.copyright.com.au), no part of this publication
may be reproduced, stored in a retrieval system, transmitted,
broadcast or communicated in any form or by any means,
optical, digital, electronic, mechanical, photocopying, recording
or otherwise, without the written permission of the publisher.

Edited by Shaneen Goodwin
Cover design, text design and typesetting by Nada Backovic
Cover image © iStock.com/Ridofranz

Paperback ISBN 9781923569126
ePub ISBN 9781923569133

A catalogue record for this book is available from the National Library of Australia.

FOREWORD

> *Research is revealing the powerful impact that school leadership teams can have in improving the quality of teaching and learning. Effective leaders create cultures of high expectations, provide clarity about what teachers are to teach and students are to learn, establish strong professional learning communities and lead ongoing efforts to improve teaching practices. (Masters 2012)*

School leadership is an increasingly complex, highly demanding role. School leaders are accountable for a broad range of factors and outcomes and to a wide array of stakeholders. In establishing short- and long-term goals for improving outcomes for students, school leaders must turn their minds not only to performance indicators and targets but to the methods, approaches and strategies through which those targets can be achieved.

Research tells us that schools and school systems that embrace evidence-based practice models are those most likely to achieve their goals of improving outcomes for young people. It also tells us that it is school leaders who play a critical role in identifying, implementing, embedding and leading evidence-based practice.

The 'High impact strategies for school leaders' series is designed as a resource for those busy school leaders whose ultimate aim is to improve outcomes for all learners. Each book in the series, focusing on a different domain within the school environment, unpacks for school leaders the ways high-impact strategies and practices can be applied to achieve improvement goals. Written by highly regarded experts in their fields, the series seeks to focus attention on the role of school leaders in driving the processes that result in effective school and classroom practice and improved outcomes for students and help them navigate through the dizzying array of information about 'what works' and what doesn't.

In *Leading improvement in literacy teaching and learning*, literacy education expert Associate Professor Robyn Cox presents a range of evidenced-informed practices that can be used as a focus for teacher professional learning and school improvement, aligning each of these with high-impact teaching strategies. Cox also highlights the role of principals and other school-based leaders in leading teaching and learning and suggests that whole-school approaches are among the most successful strategies.

Robyn Cox specialises in language and literacy education and has particular expertise in initial teacher education in teaching early reading. Cox brings this wealth of knowledge to *Leading improvement in literacy teaching and learning and* provides research evidence and practical tools to support 5 key literacy practices in schools, including teaching oral language, teaching grammar and writing, explicit vocabulary instruction, teaching early reading and intervention and support for literacy learners. In addition, an introductory chapter unpacks the role of evidence in determining what a 'high-impact practice' is within school and classroom environments.

Cox draws on some of her own well-received research and the work of other educational authorities in constructing the set of 5 high-impact literacy practices that shape this book. Together, these provide an effective framework for schools and school leaders to strengthen their literacy teaching practices and student outcomes.

CONTENTS

Foreword		v
Acknowledgements		xi
Chapter 1	**High-impact practices: the role of evidence**	**1**
	Introduction	1
	What is evidence?	3
	What are data?	4
	What is research?	6
	What is methodology?	7
	What is high-impact practice?	10
	What counts as evidence in schools and classrooms?	10
	Ethics	16
	Theory	17
	Evidence-based practice in the classroom: challenges	19
	Linking teaching practices to research	24
	References	29
Chapter 2	**Oral language**	**35**
	Introduction	35
	How oral language development can support achievement in literacy	35
	Strategies to help literacy achievement in your school	38

	Reflections from school leaders	47
	School-wide improvement	49
	Annotated bibliography	50
	References	51
Chapter 3	**Teaching grammar and writing**	**55**
	Introduction	55
	How explicit teaching of grammar can support achievement in literacy and writing	58
	Strategies to help literacy achievement in your school	64
	Reflections from school leaders	68
	School-wide improvement	70
	Annotated bibliography	72
	References	73
Chapter 4	**Explicit vocabulary instruction**	**77**
	Introduction	77
	How explicit vocabulary instruction can support achievement in literacy	78
	Strategies to help literacy achievement in your school	82
	Reflections from school leaders	86
	School-wide improvement	91
	Annotated bibliography	93
	References	94

Chapter 5	Teaching early reading	97
	Introduction	97
	How the explicit teaching of reading can support achievement in literacy	98
	Strategies to help literacy achievement in your school	106
	Reflections from school leaders	111
	School-wide improvement	112
	Annotated bibliography	115
	References	117
Chapter 6	Intervention and supporting literacy learners	121
	Introduction	121
	How diagnostic assessment and tailored intervention can support achievement in literacy	122
	Strategies to help literacy achievement in your school	133
	Reflections from school leaders	137
	School-wide improvement	140
	References	142
Chapter 7	Conclusion	145
	References	150

ACKNOWLEDGEMENTS

An earlier version of Chapter 1 appeared as:

Feez S and Cox R (2017) *PEN 209 Understanding research & evidence: a teachers guide*, Primary English Teaching Association Australia (PETAA), Newtown, NSW.

I would like to acknowledge Susan Feez with whom I co-authored the above guide, and the Primary English Teaching Association Australia (PETAA) for providing permission for the reuse of the material.

Thanks are also due to Helen West, David Partridge, Monica Palmer, Sandra Armstrong and Imogene Cochrane Bond. These are the school leaders who provide the insightful reflections in this book about their experiences with school-based high-impact practices in literacy teaching and learning.

CHAPTER 1

High-impact practices: the role of evidence

Introduction

Recently, I was driving on a NSW country road listening to an ABC radio interview with Dr Fiona Stanley, who is an Australian epidemiologist noted for her public health work. Dr Stanley was Australian of the Year in 2003 for her work in paediatric public health over many decades. In the interview, Dr Stanley consistently reiterated the phrase 'causal pathways' – for her, the evidence from the many studies into child health in her area of expertise demonstrated the 'causal pathways' for public health. This got me thinking about this book. In education and particularly in literacy education, do we have such clearly defined 'causal pathways'? Perhaps we do. We will revisit this at the conclusion of this book.

Demands in recent decades for school leaders to implement evidence-based decision-making and practice in their classrooms (Centre for Education Statistics and Evaluation 2014; Matters 2006) have been growing. There have even been suggestions to restrict the practice of teachers to approaches identified as evidence-based (Bruniges 2005).

When decisions are made to implement a pedagogical approach, which is informed by research evidence, teaching is said to be 'evidence based'. There is, however, much debate about what counts as evidence, which evidence is most relevant to specific teaching contexts and student profiles, how teachers should apply evidence to their practice, and how school leaders should support evidence-based practice. This chapter provides teachers and school leaders with knowledge they can use to:

> reflect on what counts as evidence in relation to literacy education

> evaluate the relevance and strength of evidence derived from different research methodologies to their own practice

> consider how to apply different types of evidence in their teaching context.

School leaders have become accustomed to enthusiasts promoting new educational approaches they claim will lead to gains in student achievement. For this reason, school leaders need to critically evaluate claims that a particular practice is 'evidence based'. They need to ensure that such claims are not merely contributing to the endless stream of novel, but often ephemeral, trends that are routinely visited on school leaders, teachers and their students.

Evidence-based teaching is most commonly promoted by those who argue that teaching programs should be based on evidence derived from research designed using scientific experimental methods to generate reliable evidence that can help improve decision-making and practice (Hempenstall 2006; Wyatt-Smith and Gunn 2007). The value of this type of evidence for teachers, however, has been called into question by those arguing that experimental methods designed to investigate natural processes are less valid and reliable when applied to cultural and social processes, such as teaching and learning. In educational contexts, double-blind studies, random selection of participants and control of variables are rarely possible, unless they are used to measure the development of limited, or constrained, sets of skills or knowledge that can be learnt relatively quickly (Freebody 2007, 2010; Paris and Luo 2010; Taber 2013).

Nevertheless, a consensus is emerging among educators that 'a sound basis for action is converging evidence from multiple sources and different perspectives' because '[e]vidence-based convergence lends strength to findings as no single study, methodology, finding or view is considered, in and of itself, a sufficient basis for action' (Wyatt-Smith et al. 2011: 3). This view is supported by Myhill (2016: 321), who argues that 'the most robust evidence comes from an accumulation of studies, preferably including replication studies conducted by others'.

The term 'evidence' is used routinely, but not always precisely, to promote particular teaching practices, alongside terms such as 'research', 'data' and 'methodology'. These terms are explored below.

What is evidence?

The word 'evidence' has its origin in the Latin word *videre*, which means 'to see', the same origin as words such as 'visible' and 'vision'. The *e-* at the beginning of evidence is from the Latin prefix *ex-*, meaning 'out of'. So, evidence emerges out of what we can see. Because evidence is something that has been seen, and so verified, it can be used to support a claim or assertion that something is true.

In the legal system, during a criminal trial, lawyers for the prosecution will present evidence, perhaps physical evidence gathered by investigators or evidence provided by witnesses, to support their case that the defendant is guilty. Lawyers representing the defendant will produce evidence to support the opposite view. The task of the trial judge and jury is to weigh up the evidence before coming to a decision about the guilt or otherwise of the defendant. A comparable task falls to school leaders as they decide whether to provide the resources and support needed to implement a particular practice in their school.

In the field of science, scientists answer their questions and test their theories about natural phenomena by gathering empirical evidence. Empirical evidence is evidence that can be perceived by the senses. It is made up of data collected through observation, experiment and/or measurement. The data are interpreted through statistical analysis, and evidence obtained in this way can be further tested, and ideally, reproduced. Techniques for collecting, analysing and interpreting data to produce evidence vary from one field of academic inquiry to the next.

Part of the task for school leaders when weighing up evidence is to find out which techniques from which field of academic inquiry were used to analyse the data, and to make judgements about the relevance of these research techniques to their teaching situation.

What are data?

The word 'data' is the plural form of the Latin word *datum*, which means 'something given'. In a scientific study, each piece of information, for instance each observation or each measurement, is one datum. When these pieces of information are collected together, they are called 'data', a word that in academic English is used as a plural noun indicating that each piece of information can be counted. In everyday English, however, data is commonly used as a singular noun, referring to information as a single 'mass' rather than as separate countable items.

Controlled experiments are designed so a researcher can isolate and test the impact of a single 'independent variable'. While all other variables are held constant ('controlled variables'), the independent variable is adjusted and/or used as a treatment or intervention. Data are collected by observing, measuring and/or recording the effects of this treatment or intervention.

Data can also be collected under less controlled conditions including in the field, for example, in classrooms. Data collection can be undertaken by participants in the setting or activity under investigation, or by observers looking on, who are not participating. Examples of data that can be collected in educational settings include:

> formal or informal observations, recorded as field notes, in a diary, daybook or journal, in a graphic organiser, or against a checklist

> photographs, audio or video recordings

- artefacts such as samples of student work, including spoken and written texts, models, demonstrations, presentations and illustrations
- responses to surveys, questionnaires and interviews
- contributions to conferences and focus groups
- 'maps' or charts, for example, classroom or playground layout, student movement, sociogram of student interaction
- measurement, such as of time taken, distance or area covered, tasks completed, attendance, marks achieved in quizzes, tests, term assignments and end of year examinations, or national test scores (for example, NAPLAN), and assessments against scales (such as, of attitudes).

When patterns are found in the data, and these are interpreted, data become information. Information organised in an abstract, systematic way so that it can be generalised, transferred and/or reapplied productively in other contexts becomes evidence.

It is interesting for school leaders to consider which elements of student progress can be counted or measured in some way, and which cannot. School attendance and test scores, for example, can be counted or measured, and expressed as quantitative data. Records of classroom observation, lesson study, student performance or interviews with students and parents, perhaps captured in the form of notes, photographs, audio-visual recordings or work samples, are qualitative data. This leads to questions about how relations between teaching practice and student progress that cannot be easily measured or recorded might be evaluated. It also calls into question the relationship between measurements that produce quantitative data and observations or data sets that produce qualitative data. Are some stronger than the others and do they carry more weight in decision-making?

What is research?

Research, according to Dörnyei (2007: 15), simply means 'trying to find answers to questions'. Researchers can find answers to their questions by undertaking an original investigation ('primary research') or by searching for what other researchers have already found ('secondary research'). Typically, an original investigation begins with secondary research, such as a literature review, to find out what is already known and where the gaps are in our knowledge, followed by primary research to gather data that can be used to help answer questions to fill the knowledge gaps. Primary research can be an experimental and/or theoretical investigation to build new knowledge ('pure basic research'), to solve a practical problem ('strategic basic research'), or to build knowledge for a specific application or to achieve one or more specified objectives ('applied research').

Most educational research is applied research, undertaken to improve learning outcomes for students. Applied research in education draws on theories from a range of academic disciplines, for example, psychology, sociology, linguistics and history. What counts as evidence, and how it is collected, analysed, interpreted and shared with others, varies from one discipline to the next. This presents a challenge for teachers striving to ensure their practice is evidence based. This variation also presents a challenge for school leaders working with teachers whose views about what counts as evidence may differ, depending on their background discipline knowledge, their initial teacher education, their professional learning and the access they have to reputable academic and professional publications.

Evidence emerging from applied education research is shared with others in papers presented at conferences, and in books, journal articles and reports. Reputable publications of this type are blind peer reviewed. In other words, for a study to be reported in a reputable publication, it must first be evaluated by scholars and/or practitioners with relevant knowledge and expertise who do not know who carried out the study. The peer review process provides assurance that the methodology used to produce the evidence meets standards accepted by the discipline and/or profession.

What is methodology?

A methodology is a systematic and principled approach, or framework, used by a researcher to design a study to answer research questions. This approach will usually include a theoretical framework and a set of techniques and methods, which can be either 'quantitative' or 'qualitative'. Quantitative and qualitative methods can be combined in mixed- or multi-method studies.

Quantitative techniques are used to gather data, potentially very large quantities of data, which can be measured and analysed using statistics. In the sciences, experiments under laboratory conditions are designed to maximise the degree to which variables can be controlled, the experiment can be repeated, and the findings can be generalised. The type of experiment described as the 'gold standard' of research design is the 'randomised controlled trial' (RCT). To limit the possibility of the results being skewed through bias, in randomised controlled trials, research participants are randomly assigned to either control groups or experimental groups. Ideally, researchers as well as participants are 'blind' to the way the participants are assigned to each group. The control group is not subjected to the treatment or intervention being tested on an experimental group, so the control group becomes the 'baseline' for comparison to determine the relative effectiveness of the treatment or treatments applied to one or more experimental groups. In the social sciences, quantitative research often involves the statistical analysis of large-scale survey responses and test results.

Qualitative techniques are used in the social sciences to gather data through observation, and record keeping, and by interpreting what people participating in the research do or say. Because qualitative research typically investigates human experience in social contexts, it is much more difficult to control variables. This problem can be overcome to some extent by using the same techniques used to collect quantitative data, in which participants are randomly assigned to separate control and intervention groups, and by ensuring the study is double blind, that is, neither the researcher nor the participants know who is in which group while the intervention is happening. If the research is being undertaken with one particular group, for example, a case study of students in one classroom, the study is considered to be quasi-experimental, and the findings not as reliable. Methodologies and related data collection and analytical techniques used in some exemplar literacy education studies are listed in Box 1.1.

Box 1.1. Methodologies, research and data collection techniques used in exemplar literacy education studies

Meta-analysis
Research technique: quantitative
Data collection: reviewing and collating statistically the results of multiple quantitative studies
Exemplar study: Hattie J (2009) *Visible learning: a meta-analysis of 800 meta-analyses relating to achievement*, Routledge, Oxford, UK.

Random controlled trials
Research technique: quantitative
Data collection: conducting double blind studies, large scale experiments
Exemplar studies: Buckingham J, Beaman-Wheldall R and Wheldall K (2012) 'A randomised control trial of a MultiLit small group intervention for older low-progress readers', *Effective Education*, 4(1):1–26.
Myhill D, Jones S, Lines H and Watson A (2012) 'Re-thinking grammar: the impact of embedded grammar teaching on students' writing and students' metalinguistic understanding', *Research Papers in Education*, 27(2):139–166.

Standardised instruments
Research technique: quantitative
Data collection: conducting surveys, tests, questionnaires
Exemplar study: Invernizzi M, Sullivan A, Meier J and Swank, L (2004) *The Phonological Awareness Literacy Screening for Preschool (PALS)*, University of Virginia, Charlottesville, VA.

Discourse analysis
Research technique: qualitative, quantitative, mixed methods
Data collection: analysing classroom discourse, multimodal and/or written texts
Exemplar study: Christie F and Derewianka B (2008) *School discourse: learning to write across the years of schooling*, Continuum, London.

Verbal protocols

Research technique: qualitative, quantitative
Data collection: recalling and thinking aloud while performing a task
Exemplar study: Young KA (2005) 'Direct from the source: the value of "think aloud" data in understanding learning', *Journal of Educational Enquiry*, 6(1):19–33.

Action and design-based research

Research technique: qualitative, quantitative, mixed methods
Data collection: investigating problems and intervening iteratively to resolve a problem
Exemplar studies: Edwards-Groves C and Davidson C (2017) *Becoming a meaning maker: talk and interaction in the dialogic classroom*, Primary English Teaching Association (PETAA), Newtown, NSW.
Parkin B and Harper H (2018) *Teaching with intent: scaffolding academic language with marginalised students*, Primary English Teaching Association (PETAA), Newtown, NSW.

Case studies

Research technique: qualitative, quantitative, mixed methods
Data collection: including instrumental, collective and multiple case studies
Exemplar study: Hill S, Comber B, Louden W and Reid J (2002) *100 children turn 10: a longitudinal study of literacy development from the year prior to school to the first four years of school*, Commonwealth Department of Science, Education and Training, Canberra.

Ethnography

Research technique: qualitative, quantitative
Data collection: undertaking interviews, observations, producing documents to build descriptions of social practices
Exemplar study: Heath SB (1983) *Ways with words: language, life and work in communities and classrooms*, Cambridge University Press, Cambridge.

What is high-impact practice?

High-impact practices are teaching and learning practices that have been widely tested and have been shown to be beneficial for learners from different backgrounds. These practices take many forms, depending on learner characteristics and on school and system priorities. We often say that a high-impact practice is demonstrated when teaching and learning practices are studied, widely tested and evaluated to produce evidence of the kind described earlier. The chapters in this book include descriptions of 5 high-impact practices that educational research suggests have a positive effect on student learning. The evidence supporting each of these practices is reviewed from the perspective of the research design, the data collected, and the methods used.

What counts as evidence in schools and classrooms?

How can school leaders evaluate the evidence used to claim that a particular teaching approach, strategy or program is effective? The first step is to consider whether the evidence is strong or weak.

ANECDOTAL EVIDENCE

In a school, if a teacher tries out a strategy or implements a program once or twice, and the students are engaged and demonstrate improvement in their learning, the teacher is likely to share their experience of the success of that strategy or program with colleagues. 'Anecdotal evidence' of this type, however, is considered to be weak. While it is always worth learning from our colleagues' accounts of successful professional practice, we cannot be sure how or why the practice was successful, or whether successful implementation of the practice could be repeated with different students by a different teacher at a different time.

ACTION RESEARCH

'Action research' is a form of enquiry school leaders and teachers can use to understand their work practices and how their work impacts on their students and/or colleagues. Action research is a systematic way for teachers to reflect on their practice, and to investigate questions about how to improve it (Burns 2010). It has been described by Kemmis et al. (2014: 4) as a type of research 'oriented to making improvements in practices and their settings by the participants themselves'.

Through action research, school leaders can evaluate and improve their practice by examining successes to understand how and why they worked and by investigating challenges and problems with the goal of improving learning outcomes. The action research process begins when the researcher formulates a question, for example, When I do this, why does that improve, but the other does not? How can I improve . . .? To answer the question, the researcher designs an action research plan. The design of the plan will incorporate:

> informed action, that is, a principled change to the teaching context or teaching practice with the goal of improving learning outcomes

> procedures for collecting data before, during and afterwards

> procedures for reflecting on and interpreting the data to revise the plan and to inform the next action in the cycle.

The action research plan must be practical and achievable in the teaching context. The first step is the collection of 'baseline data', that is, data collected before any action is taken. The second step is to implement action, recording the effect. The teacher then reflects on what happened to revise and plan for the next action in the series. The data collected during each 'action – evaluation – reflection' cycle is called 'in-cycle data'. The evidence that emerges from action research findings can be used as evidence to support changes in classroom practice. These changes then need to be monitored to see if they continue to have a positive impact on the learning outcomes of the students in the class over time. The findings can be shared with colleagues, who might trial the same or similar actions, or the findings might be used to generate further questions to investigate.

When teachers undertake action research, they often collaborate with university researchers. University researchers can assist with the design of the action research and systematic data collection, as well as the use of theoretical concepts to analyse and interpret the data and to enhance the strength of the evidence emerging from the project. University researchers can also assist with the publication of findings, so these are shared more widely, and can become a starting point for classroom-based innovation and research elsewhere.

DESIGN-BASED RESEARCH

Another methodology used for research collaborations by school leaders, teachers and university academics is known as 'design-based research', involving 'small, pragmatic, planned and classroom data-informed interventions, designed with the intention of developing theory about and demonstrating evidence of effective literacy pedagogic practice' (Comber et al. 2016: 316). This methodology has been developed to blend 'empirical educational research with the theory-driven design of learning environments'. It has been described as 'an important methodology for understanding how, when and why educational innovations work in practice', and as the relation between theory and practice (The Design-based Research Collective 2003: 5). The aim of this type of research is to 'create usable knowledge', while at the same time advancing 'theories of learning and teaching in complex settings' (The Design-based Research Collective 2003: 5).

Design-based research is made up of a series of 'designed pedagogical experiments and . . . interventions in iterative cycles' (Comber et al. 2016: 318). Data is collected and analysed, and, on that basis, the pedagogies and interventions are modified before being implemented again in the next cycle. '[Design-based research] means that teachers collect baseline performance data on an area of students' learning they are wanting to improve, design and implement a pedagogical intervention informed by theory and related research, and subsequently collect another set of student performance data to compare with the first' (Freebody and Morgan 2014: 9).

When university researchers and school leaders collaborate to improve practice and to generate evidence of effective practice, the design of the project must account for both the ethics of using students as research participants, and the theory to be applied as a tool for organising, thinking about and interpreting the data.

CASE STUDIES

To examine more closely the potential effectiveness of a teaching practice in an actual teaching situation with a specific group of students, the implementation of the practice might be carefully and systematically recorded and described in detail from the planning stage to final assessment of student achievement. A 'case study' of this type often begins with an ethnographic description, that is, a systematic description of the wider context in which the practice is being implemented, including the cultural and social circumstances of the students and their families, the curriculum context and the teaching situation, the age of the students, their stage of development and their learning needs.

In educational research, the 'case' being studied might be a particular teaching practice or program, a teaching intervention, the progress made by a single student, one whole class or school of a particular profile (a single case), or a group of students, multiple classes or schools of comparable or diverse profiles (a multiple case).

A case study can include the use of quantitative and qualitative methods, and can be used to illustrate, evaluate, explain and/or explore a teaching practice or program of interest in a particular context. A case study can also be used as a pilot study in preparation for undertaking a study on a much larger scale (Mills et al. 2010; Yin 2014).

Case study evidence is not considered by some to be strong because it is not based on data drawn from a very large population, and so cannot be used for statistical generalisation. Nevertheless, evidence based on a case studied in context has the potential to be transferred to other comparable contexts (Jensen 2008). Case study evidence can also be used to challenge generalisations based on evidence emerging from large-scale experimental studies, and to question whether a general finding is applicable in specific contexts of interest.

STANDARDISED TESTING

Evidence drawn from standardised testing of large student populations is considered as strong evidence. In Australia, the National Assessment Program: Literacy and Numeracy (NAPLAN) comprises a collection of standardised tests designed to assess whether Australian students are achieving minimum outcomes in foundation skills of reading, writing, language and numeracy at key stages of schooling. To ensure students are tested as consistently as possible, all aspects of the delivery of the test are standardised, including the design of the test items, the conditions under which students sit the tests, and the way student responses are scored and interpreted. In recent years, the NAPLAN tests have been administered online, thus ensuring the conditions of sitting the tests are strongly controlled through using technology.

NAPLAN results provide a snapshot of what each child, class of students, year group, school, sector, system or region, and the national cohort, can achieve on one day when tested for a limited set of skills and knowledge. Because the test is standardised, student performance at each of these levels, and across time, can be compared. The findings can be used by parents, teachers, schools, systems and funding providers to track progress and to identify where intervention and/or extra resources might be needed. NAPLAN is also promoted as a means for making teachers and schools more accountable.

Although NAPLAN tests are standardised and NAPLAN data are collected from a large population at regular intervals, the statistical reliability of the data, and comparability of the results from one year to the next, and from one individual, school or sector to the next, have been questioned. In other words, despite NAPLAN being a large-scale standardised test, there are differing opinions about the strength of the evidence supplied by NAPLAN, and how much it can be relied upon to guide decisions about teaching practice. Moreover, because NAPLAN is a single snapshot of a limited range of skills, it does not reflect student achievement across all areas of the curriculum, which raises questions about the validity of some of the ways NAPLAN data are used (see Wu 2016). While the purpose of NAPLAN is to improve teaching and learning because NAPLAN is becoming increasingly high stakes for teachers and schools, 'much teaching is now aimed at improving NAPLAN scores' (Lingard et al. 2016: 6). This has the potential perverse effect of narrowing the curriculum and reducing the capacity of teachers and schools for differentiating the curriculum to meet the diverse learning needs of students.

EXPERIMENTAL METHODS

Evidence that is statistically the strongest is based on data collected using experimental methods, such as randomised controlled trials in which participants are assigned randomly to separate control and experimental groups. As described earlier, all variables are controlled, and kept constant, except for one, which, in the experimental group, is deliberately manipulated. The responses of participants in both groups are measured and data collected from the 2 groups are compared using statistical analysis during which the 'effect size' of manipulating the one variable is calculated for significance. Experiments of this type are designed so they can be repeated in exactly the same way, with the potential for strengthening the evidence even more. Experimental findings emerging from randomised controlled trials are promoted as delivering the strongest evidence for the effectiveness, or not, of a particular teaching strategy or practice (Kamil 2012) because the evidence is considered to be generalisable.

The evidence becomes even stronger when results from multiple studies of a similar or related type are collected and collated. This is achieved when researchers undertake a systematic review or meta-analysis. A systematic review, for example, a literature review, is a review and synthesis of evidence gathered from a selection of related studies (see Chall 1967; Freebody 2007; Snow et al. 1998). A meta-analysis is the use of statistical methods to synthesise the results of related studies, often to compare the effect sizes of different treatments or interventions (see Hattie 2009; Myhill and Watson 2014).

While experimental evidence is understood to be the strongest and most rigorously derived evidence available, 'maintaining true experimental or even quasi-experimental designs' has 'often been impossible ... in the world of schools' (Schwandt et al. 2007: 15). One reason for this is that schools and classrooms are complex social contexts in which the many variables 'are interrelated in such a way as to influence all other' variables (Schwandt et al. 2007: 17). Measuring one variable isolated under experimental conditions may not predict accurately the effect of that same variable in a classroom context. Similarly, 'what children do . . . under experimental conditions' may be 'very little guide' to what they do in classrooms (Halliday 2007: 184).

To maintain rigour, experimental studies are designed to ensure the evidence is 'valid' (a true generalisable representation), 'reliable' (consistent) and 'objective' (unbiased). A corresponding framework proposed for the design of studies undertaken in social settings is based on the notion of trustworthiness to ensure that evidence is credible and transferable, dependable and neutral (Schwandt et al. 2007).

Ethics

The ethics of designing classroom-based research must be transparent, practical, valid, reliable and authentic. In addition, researchers must account for the fact that the relationship between students and teachers is not an equal one, so they must ensure the research has 'merit and integrity', is justifiable, respectful, of potential benefit, in the best interests of the students, and safe, thus, protecting the students' physical, emotional and psychological wellbeing (National Health and Medical Research Council 2007: 29-31). Before participating in research, students, and their parents for those under 18, must give their consent. Because educators are in a position of authority, classroom-based research is designed in ways that ensure parental and student consent is informed and freely given. Parents and students need to be assured that there will be no negative consequences if they decline to participate or choose to withdraw at any time.

Research involving children and young people raises particular ethical concerns about:

> their capacity to understand what the research entails, and therefore whether their consent to participate is sufficient for their participation

> their possible coercion by parents, peers, researchers or others to participate in research

> conflicting values and interests of parents and children.
(National Health and Medical Research Council 2007: 29)

Theory

To organise, think about and interpret data, researchers use 'theory'. In everyday language, we often use the word theory when we are talking about possibilities or guesses, for example, 'In theory, we should be able to win this.' Researchers, on the other hand, use the term theory to label the conceptual and theoretical frameworks, body of knowledge, or model they use to organise, explain and interpret data. A theory is like a map the researcher uses to find their way around the research context and the data, and to locate different elements in relation to each other.

Practitioners often dismiss theory as not relevant to resolving their day-to-day challenges and problems. Nevertheless, working from a sound theory or model enables practitioners to reflect on their practice systematically and critically. It also allows them to generalise based on reflective practice to sustain successful innovations over time and to implement innovative ideas emerging from their findings in different contexts.

Figure 1.1 demonstrates a view of the strength of evidence when the type of research methodology is taken into consideration. Of course, this is highly contestable, and the figure is only here to provide ease of reflection when school leaders are reviewing research findings in the following chapters.

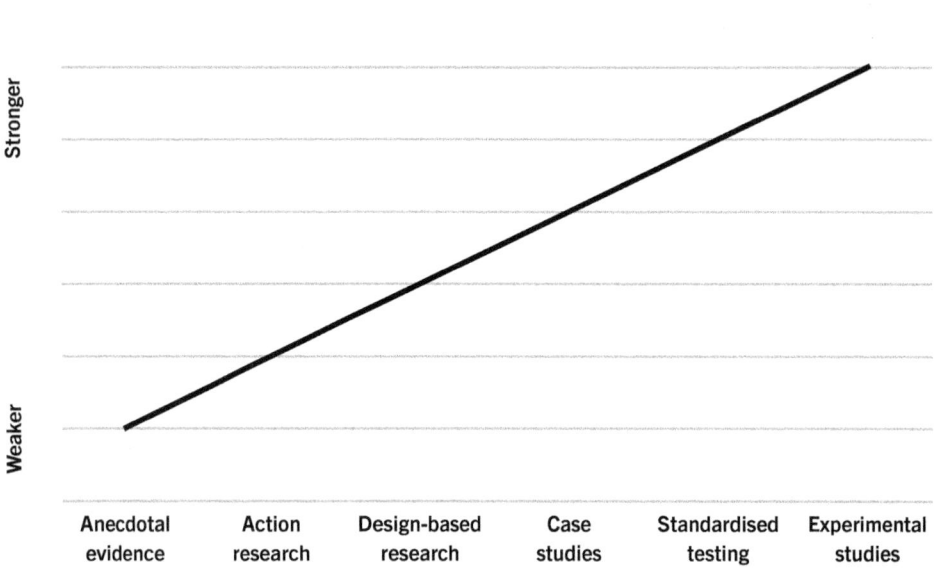

Figure 1.1. Comparative strength of types of evidence

The idea that good theory and good practice depend on each other has echoed through the centuries. This is illustrated in the following maxims, the first by Leonardo da Vinci in the fifteenth century, and the second, in the twentieth century, by Kurt Lewin, who coined the term 'action research'.

> *Those who fall in love with practice without science [knowledge/ theory] are like a sailor who enters a ship without a helm or a compass, and who never can be certain whither he is going. (The Notebooks of Leonardo da Vinci, Chapter XIX)*
>
> *There's nothing so practical as a good theory. (Lewin 1951: 169)*

Evidence-based practice in the classroom: challenges

Particular types of instruction are often promoted by educational policymakers and administrators, and commercial interests, as evidence based in ways that imply the approach works for all students in all contexts. Now that we have read and considered the elements of research design and the relative strength of research findings, school leaders should be able to decide for themselves. There are still complexities around 'what works' and even when a teaching strategy or practice is promoted as being 'evidence based', school leaders should make professional judgements about whether and how the strategy or practice should be applied in their contexts.

The following section provides a series of tools and heuristics for school leaders to apply when they want to be sure that the high-impact practices that they are promoting do indeed come from a sound evidence base.

To make such judgements, school leaders can ask questions such as:

Transparency	Can the practice be implemented in a way that ensures students are clear about what is expected of them and why?
Practicality	Does the benefit of implementing this practice outweigh any burden it might place on teachers and students in terms of time, effort and stress?
Validity	Is the evidence on which the claimed benefit of this practice is based meaningful in this specific teaching context, or are the claims unrelated or overstated in relation to the needs of this particular group of students?
Reliability	Will the evidence on which the claimed benefit of this practice is based hold true for this group of students and in this teaching and learning context at this time?
Authenticity	Does the practice address the real-world demands of the curriculum and the learning needs of this group of students? Does it enable the students to engage meaningfully with curriculum content and will it help them meet their long-term educational needs and goals?

With the heavy promotion of teaching practices labelled as 'evidence based' by policymakers and commercial interests, school leaders and teachers need to become critical consumers of this type of promotion. They need to apply their professional judgement in ways such as those described above to weigh up competing and contradictory claims, and to avoid 'cherry-picking' from the evidence to support a certain agenda, or one side of a debate.

When evidence derived from research designed using experimental methods is tempered by evidence emerging from research designed using ethnographic, case study and text analysis methods, the distinctive features of specific teaching contexts and student profiles can be accounted for.

> Can teachers in real-world settings faithfully replicate the evidence-based teaching strategy?

> Has the evidence collected by researchers to underpin claims that a teaching practice or strategy is evidence based been adjusted to account for diverse real-life classroom settings; for example, through accompanying ethnographic and field descriptions, systematic observation and/or text analysis?

> Can teaching resources used in the experimental studies be made available and relevant, or accurately replicated in specific real-world settings?

Researchers themselves have pointed out the rarefied nature of educational research, where researchers may be able to control variables in the design of experimental studies used to evaluate a teaching approach, but classroom teachers are rarely afforded this luxury (Freebody 2007; See also Fehring and Freebody 2017; Proctor et al. 2015). In classrooms:

> ethnographic studies, which document the social context in which the research takes place, may produce evidence that school leaders and teachers find more

accessible because it more closely reflects their classroom experience (Purcell-Gates et al. 2011)

› while case study findings may not represent large populations, and so cannot be used statistically to make generalised claims, the findings of a case study that includes a detailed description of the teaching and learning context can be transferred to comparable contexts (Jensen 2008)

› when student work samples are analysed using principled frameworks (a theory) for describing consistently the way students respond to the language and literacy demands of the curriculum, the analysis can reveal which aspects of language and literacy development are key to meeting those demands and suggest teaching practices that might contribute to student progress (Derewianka and Jones 2016; Humphrey et al. 2012)

› principled frameworks also provide shared tools for assessment, and for comparing the language and literacy demands of different educational contexts, identifying the distinct language and literacy demands of specialised learning areas, such as science or history, and understanding the way multimodal and digital texts make meaning (Callow 2013; Derewianka 2011; Derewianka and Jones 2016; Humphrey et al. 2012; Polias 2016).

WHERE PROFESSIONAL JUDGEMENT MEETS RESEARCH EVIDENCE

Early literacy

An area of English teaching in which teachers must use professional judgement to navigate competing research agendas and high-profile debates is the teaching of early literacy (Feez 2019). The experimental evidence is very strong that intensive systematic instruction in the sounds of English (phonemic awareness) and their correspondence with the letters of the English alphabet (phonics) has a positive effect on the English word reading skills of children in the early years of school (see Buckingham et al. 2013; Buckingham et al. 2019), and to some extent prevents later reading difficulties (Ehri et al. 2001). As a result, this type of instruction is now heavily promoted, with phonics screening tests being mandated in many states in Australia.

When the high-stakes spotlight is on teaching practices designed to teach sound–letter correspondence (code-breaking), there is a risk that less attention is paid to other critical aspects of learning to read, such as building vocabulary and reading for meaning, as well as using and interpreting the meanings socially and culturally (Freebody 2007). To counteract this risk, school leaders need to be mindful when designing literacy programs that the research evidence also shows the following:

> The ability of children to attend to speech units larger than phonemes (for example, syllables, onset and rime) is a reliable indicator of future reading success (Goswami 2006). Morphological awareness, that is, awareness of the meaningful parts of words, is also associated with improved reading comprehension (Anderson et al. 2019; Bowers and Bowers 2017; Kirby and Bowers 2017; Kirby et al. 2012).

> To learn to read effectively, 'children need a balanced instructional approach that includes learning to break the code and engaging in meaningful reading and writing' (Xue and Meisels 2004: 222).

> To be successful throughout the school years, students need to be taught explicitly and cumulatively how to meet the advanced literacy demands of each content area (Freebody 2019; Freebody and Morgan 2014; Shanahan and Shanahan 2014).

> There are 'differences in the developmental trajectories of different reading skills' (Paris and Luo 2010: 321). Unconstrained skills like reading comprehension develop more slowly, compared to constrained skills, such as decoding, which are learnt relatively quickly (See also Luke and Woods 2008).

With a diverse array of research findings such as these, the task facing teachers of early literacy, and their school leaders, is to survey the research to design a meaningful collection of practices that make 'specific and particular sense for each group of students with whom they work' (Honan 2004: 37). This involves 'carefully and thoughtfully' making 'a series of professional judgements about what and how to teach' (Honan 2004: 39). To assemble literacy teaching practices in a principled way, teachers can use the 'four resources' model (Honan 2004: 45). The 'four resources' model can be used to organise literacy resources and practices into 4 categories:

1. resources used to break the code

2. resources used to comprehend and participate in the meanings of texts

3. resources for using texts to meet 'sociocultural expectations' (Freebody 2004: 7)

4. resources for analysing texts to reveal and challenge the predispositions and biases of the writer (Freebody 2019).

This model is a conceptual tool teachers and school leaders can use to fill 'the gaps in the map of practices they have created' (Honan 2004: 45) and, thus, to design a comprehensive and balanced literacy program.

Standardised tests

Teachers and school leaders also need to apply professional judgement, and account for the specific circumstances and needs of their students, when interpreting data emerging from all types of high-stakes testing (Goss et al. 2015; Taber 2013). They need to consider what each high-stake test is designed to assess, how it is constructed, how test results are used and the effects of testing, both positive and negative, on their students and school community (Lingard et al. 2016).

Large scale data, collected through NAPLAN for example, can be useful for tracking national, state and sector trends in the development of narrow sets of skills, and where resources need to be targeted. They are less useful, however, for understanding the educational progress and achievement of individual students and classes or for evaluating the professional knowledge and skills of individual teachers. While NAPLAN data have 'some positive uses', classroom teachers and school leaders must also account for evidence of potential 'negative impacts on learning and on student wellbeing' (Wyn et al. 2014: 6). These include narrowing the curriculum, teaching to the test, reduced student motivation to learn, increased teacher and student stress, labelling students based on deficits, a reduced emphasis on equity and social justice, and diminished capacity for teachers to differentiate their teaching to meet specific student needs (Lingard et al. 2016).

For the foreseeable future, school leaders will be working in a context in which evidence-based teaching is foregrounded, and data collected through high-stakes testing will be used to measure the performance of students, teachers, schools and school systems. This context requires educators to be critical consumers of what counts as evidence. This means recognising both the strengths and limitations of educational research, high-stakes testing, the evidence these produce and the ways this evidence is used (Lingard et al. 2016; Prain 2017; Taber 2013). Globalisation combined with the advance of information technologies has led to what has been termed the 'globalised educational reform movement' (GERM) (Sahlberg 2011) and the 'datafication' of schooling (Lingard et al. 2016).

These developments have been taken up enthusiastically by policymakers, educational administrators and commercial interests. Nevertheless, school leaders remain responsible for ensuring research evidence is used for the benefit of their students and their own professional learning.

Linking teaching practices to research

As we have mentioned already, when choosing strategies and practices to use in their classrooms, teachers must also weigh up the research evidence, both its merits and shortcomings, in relation to the complex configuration of variables that characterise each unique teaching context.

Box 1.2 takes 5 well-known teaching strategies or practices and links them to some of the research on which these are based. While this is not exhaustive, it shows some of the evidence that suggest these strategies work.

Box 1.2. Well-known classroom literacy practices: methods, findings and research

1. **A rich preschool education provides a strong foundation for future literacy development. Teachers can impact on children's literacy trajectories. Literacy development is not a neat, universal lockstep process. Some children need more time; some plateau and then race ahead.**

   ### Methods

   Longitudinal case study including standardised measures of literacy achievement, teachers as ethnographers, and purpose developed literacy assessment tasks. Importantly, the case study data were 'supported by quantitative analysis'.

   ### Findings

   Teachers could and did make a significant difference in the learning of children from low SES communities and these children can achieve significant gains when assessed using purpose developed literacy assessment tools.
   The study observed a small number of students who appeared to resist schooling and school literacies.

   ### Research evidence

   Hill S, Comber B, Louden B, Reid J and Rivalland J (1998) *100 children go to school: connections and disconnections in literacy experience prior to school and in the first year of school*, Department for Education, Employment, Training and Youth Affairs, Canberra.

2. **Collaborative classroom talk. Learners working with talking partners. Teachers plan for specific talking activities in classrooms.**

   ### Methods

   Systematic observation, computer-based text analysis, ethnographic analysis, sociolinguistic discourse analysis, conversation analysis

Findings

Identified specific ways in which classroom dialogue can promote learning and the development of understanding. Identified that specific types of talk are associated with the best learning outcomes.

Research evidence

Mercer N (2010) 'The analysis of classroom talk: methods and methodologies', *British Journal of Educational Psychology*, 80:1–14.

3. **Sustained silent reading (SSR); Drop everything and read (DEAR); Free voluntary reading (FRV); School library programs; Premier's Reading Challenge; Book week activities.**

   Methods

   Survey methods, case study methods

   Findings

   Sustained silent readers reported that they read more at the end of the SSR program than at the beginning (Pilgreen and Krashen 1993).

   Research evidence

   Pilgreen J and Krashen S (1993) 'Sustained silent reading with high school ESL students: impact on reading comprehension, reading frequency, and reading enjoyment', *School Library Media Quarterly,* 22:21–23.

4. **Text-based teaching; genre-based writing; grammar and meaning**

   Methods

   Questionnaire completed by student writers and 528 written texts collected from 33 writing situations
   Discourse analysis of 7 narrative texts written by Year 6 students

   Findings

   This doctoral study identified a model for teaching writing (deconstruction, joint construction and independent construction) that focused on language in use, rather than having traditional grammar pre-taught before writing.

Research evidence

Rothery J (1990) *Story writing in the primary school: assessing narrative type genres*, Unpublished PhD thesis, University of Sydney.

Rothery J (1996) 'Making changes: developing an educational linguistics', In Hasan R and Williams G (eds) *Literacy in society*, Longman, London.

5. **The 'big five' in reading: phonemic awareness, phonics, fluency, vocabulary, reading comprehension**

Methods

A meta-analysis of studies in the teaching of reading using these 4 criteria for inclusion:

1. Study participants must be carefully described (age; demographics; cognitive, academic, and behavioural characteristics).

2. Study interventions must be described in sufficient detail to allow for replicability, including how long the interventions lasted and how long the effects lasted.

3. Study methods must allow judgements about how instruction fidelity was ensured.

4. Studies must include a full description of outcome measures.

Findings

There are a number of research findings across the meta-analysis that have determined the 5 most important pedagogical foci for teaching early reading.

Research evidence

NICHD (National Institute of Child Health and Human Development) (2000) *Report of the National Reading Panel: teaching children to read: reports of the subgroups*. National Institute of Child Health and Human Development, National Institutes of Health, Washington, DC.

Now, read forward, armed with this knowledge, to the 5 high-impact practices examined in the next chapters. Each chapter in this book focuses on a different element of literacy and literacy teaching, examines the relevant research, presents strategies to help literacy achievement in schools, as well as considering a school-wide approach. In each area of literacy, the discussion is supported by reflections from school leaders and graphic representations of concepts. There are also several excellent commercial resources available to support school leaders in leading improvement in literacy teaching and learning. In chapters 2 to 5, some of these are highlighted in annotated bibliographies before the main reference lists.

REFERENCES

Anderson L, Whiting A, Bowers P and Venable G (2019) 'Learning to be literate: an orthographic journey with young students', in Cox R, Feez S and Beveridge L (eds) *The alphabetic principle and beyond ... surveying the landscape*, Primary English Teaching Association (PETAA), Newtown, NSW.

Bowers JS and Bowers PN (2017) 'Beyond phonics: the case for teaching children the logic of the English spelling system', *Educational Psychologist*, 52(2):124–141.

Bruniges M (2005) *An evidence-based approach to teaching and learning*, Australian Council for Educational Research (ACER), Camberwell, VIC.

Buckingham J, Wheldall K and Beaman-Wheldall R (2013) 'Why Jaydon can't read: the triumph of ideology over evidence in teaching reading', *Policy* 29(3):21–32.

Buckingham J, Wheldall K and Wheldall R (2019) 'Systematic and explicit phonics instruction: a scientific, evidence-based approach to teaching the alphabetic principle', in Cox R, Feez S and Beveridge L (eds) *The alphabetic principle and beyond ... surveying the landscape*, Primary English Teaching Association (PETAA), Newtown, NSW.

Burns A (2010) *Doing action research in English language teaching: a guide for practitioners*, Routledge, New York and London.

Callow J (2013) *The shape of text to come: how image and text work*, Primary English Teaching Association Australia (PETAA), Newtown, NSW.

Centre for Education Statistics and Evaluation (2014) *What works best: evidence-based practices to help improve NSW student performance*, Department of Education and Communities, Sydney.

Chall JS (1967) *Learning to read: the great debate*, McGraw Hill, New York.

Christie F and Derewianka B (2008) *School discourse: learning to write across the years of schooling*, Continuum, London.

Clark MM (ed) (2017) *Reading the evidence: synthetic phonics and literacy learning*, Glendale Education, Birmingham, UK.

Comber B, Freebody P, Nixon H, Carrington V and Morgan M (2016) 'New literacy demands in the middle years — learning from design experiments', in de Silva Joyce H and Feez S (eds) *Exploring literacies: theory, research and practice*, Palgrave Macmillan, London.

Derewianka B (2011) *A new grammar companion for teachers*, Primary English Teaching Association Australia (PETAA), Newtown, NSW.

Derewianka B and Jones P (2016) *Teaching language in context* (2nd edition), Oxford University Press, Melbourne.

Dörnyei Z (2007) *Research methods in applied linguistics: qualitative, quantitative and mixed methodologies*, Oxford University Press, Oxford.

Edwards-Groves C and Davidson C (2017) *Becoming a meaning maker: talk and interaction in the dialogic classroom*, Primary English Teaching Association (PETAA), Newtown, NSW.

Ehri LC, Nunes SR, Willows DM, Schuster BV, Yahgoub-Zadeh Z and Shanahan T (2001) 'Phonemic awareness instruction helps children learn to read: evidence from the National Reading Panel's meta-analysis', *Reading Research Quarterly*, 36(3):250–287.

Feez S (2019) 'The alphabetic principle: an orientation', in Cox R, Feez S and Beveridge L (eds) *The alphabetic principle and beyond ... surveying the landscape*, Primary English Teaching Association (PETAA), Newtown, NSW.

Feez S and Cox R (2017) *PEN 209 Understanding research & evidence: a teachers guide*, Primary English Teaching Association Australia (PETAA), Newtown, NSW.

Fehring H and Freebody P (2017) 'Assessment into practice: understanding assessment practice to improve students' literacy learning', in Fehring H (ed) *Assessment into practice: understanding assessment practice to improve students' literacy learning*, Primary English Teaching Association (PETAA), Newtown, NSW.

Freebody P (2004) 'Hindsight and foresight: putting the four, roles model of reading to work in the daily business of teaching', in Healy A and Honan E (eds) *Text next: new resources for literacy learning*, Primary English Teaching Association (PETAA), Newtown, NSW.

Freebody P (2007) *Literacy education in school: research perspectives from the past, for the future*, Australian Council for Educational Research (ACER), Camberwell, VIC.

Freebody P (2010) 'Socially responsible literacy education: toward an 'organic relation' to our place and time', in Christie F and Simpson A (eds) *Literacy and social responsibility: multiple perspectives*, Equinox, London & Oakville, CT.

Freebody P (2019) 'What kind of knowledge can we use? Scoping an adequate program for literacy education', in Cox R, Feez S and Beveridge L (eds) *The alphabetic principle and beyond ... surveying the landscape*, Primary English Teaching Association (PETAA), Newtown, NSW.

Freebody P and Morgan AM (2014) 'Curriculum explicit-literacy: expanding the repertoire', in Morgan AM, Comber B, Freebody P and Nixon H (eds) *Literacy in the middle years*, Primary English Teaching Association (PETAA), Newtown, NSW.

Goss P, Hunter J, Romanes D and Parsonage H (2015) *Targeted teaching: how better use of data can improve student learning*, Grattan Institute, Melbourne.

Goswami U (2006) 'Phonological awareness and literacy' *Encyclopedia of language and linguistics* (2nd Edition), Elsevier, Amsterdam.

Halliday MAK (2007) 'Language and education', in Webster JJ (ed) *Volume 9, Collected Works of M.A.K. Halliday*, Continuum, London and New York.

Hattie J (2009) *Visible learning: a synthesis of over 800 metaanalyses relating to achievement*, Routledge, London and New York.

Heath SB (1983) *Ways with words: language, life and work in communities and classrooms*, Cambridge University Press, Cambridge.

Hempenstall K (2006) What does evidence-based practice in education mean? *Australian Journal of Learning Disabilities*, 11(2):83–92.

Hill S, Comber B, Louden B, Reid J and Rivalland J (1998) *100 children go to school: connections and disconnections in literacy experience prior to school and in the first year of school*, Department for Education, Employment, Training and Youth Affairs, Canberra.

Honan E (2004) 'Using the four resources model as a map of possible practices', in Healy A and Honan E (eds) *Text next: new resources for literacy learning*, Primary English Teaching Association (PETAA), Newtown, NSW.

Humphrey S, Droga L and Feez S (2012) *Grammar and meaning*, Primary English Teaching Association (PETAA), Newtown, NSW.

Invernizzi M, Sullivan A, Meier J and Swank, L (2004) *The Phonological Awareness Literacy Screening for Preschool (PALS)*, University of Virginia, Charlottesville, VA.

Jensen D (2008) 'Transferability', in Given LM (ed) *The SAGE encyclopedia of qualitative research methods*, Sage, Thousand Oaks, CA.

Kamil ML (2012) 'Current and historical perspectives on reading research and instruction, in Harris KR, Graham S and Urdan T (eds) *APA educational psychology handbook: vol. 3. application to learning and teaching*, American Psychological Association.

Kemmis S, McTaggart R and Nixon R (2014) *The action research planner: doing critical participatory action research*, Springer, Singapore.

Kirby JR and Bowers PN (2017) 'Morphological instruction and literacy', *Theories of reading development*, 15:437.

Kirby JR, Deacon S, Bowers P, Izenberg L, Wade-Woolley L and Parrila R (2012) 'Children's morphological awareness and reading ability', *Reading & Writing*, 25(2):389–410.

Lewin K (1951) 'Problems of research in social psychology', in Cartwright D (ed) *Field theory in social science: selected theoretical papers*, Harper, New York.

Lingard B, Thompson G and Sellar S (2016) 'National testing from an Australian perspective', in Lingard B, Thompson G and Sellar S (eds) *National testing in schools: an Australian assessment*, Routledge, London and New York.

Luke A and Woods AF (2008) 'Accountability as testing: are there lessons about assessment and outcomes to be learnt from No Child Left Behind?', *Literacy Learning: The Middle Years*, 16(3):11–19.

Matters G (2006) *Using data to support learning in schools: students, teachers, systems*, Australian Council for Educational Research (ACER), Camberwell, Victoria.

Mercer N (2010) 'The analysis of classroom talk: methods and methodologies', *British Journal of Educational Psychology*, 80:1–14.

Mills A, Durepos G and Wiebe E (eds) (2010) *Encyclopedia of case study research*, Sage, Thousand Oaks, CA.

Myhill D (2016) 'Grammar for writing', in de Silva Joyce H and Feez S (eds) *Exploring literacies: theory, research and practice*, Palgrave Macmillan, London.

Myhill D, Jones S, Lines H and Watson A (2012) 'Re-thinking grammar: the impact of embedded grammar teaching on students' writing and students' metalinguistic understanding', *Research Papers in Education*, 27(2):139–166.

Myhill D and Watson A (2014) 'The role of grammar in the writing curriculum: a review of the literature', *Child Language Teaching and Therapy*, 30(1):41–62.

National Health and Medical Research Council (2007) *National statement on ethical conduct in human research* [Updated 2018], The National Health and Medical Research Council, the Australian Research Council and Universities Australia, Commonwealth of Australia, Canberra.

NELP (National Early Literacy Panel) (2008) *Developing early literacy: report of National Early Literacy Panel*, National Institute for Literacy, Washington, DC.

NICHD (National Institute of Child Health and Human Development) (2000) *Report of the National Reading Panel: teaching children to read: reports of the subgroups*, National Institute of Child Health and Human Development, National Institutes of Health, Washington, DC.

Paris SG and Luo SW (2010) 'Confounded statistical analyses hinder interpretation of the NELP report', *Educational Researcher*, 39:316–322.

Pilgreen J and Krashen S (1993) 'Sustained silent reading with high school ESL students: impact on reading comprehension, reading frequency, and reading enjoyment', *School Library Media Quarterly*, 22:21–23.

Polias J (2016) *Apprenticing students into science: doing, talking & writing scientifically*, Lexis Education, Melbourne.

Prain V and Tytler R (9 November 2017) 'Simplistic advice for teachers on how to teach won't work', *The Conversation*, accessed 28 February 2022. https://theconversation.com/simplistic-advice-for-teachers-on-how-to-teach-wont-work-86706

Proctor H, Brownlee P and Freebody P (eds) (2015) *Controversies in education: orthodoxy and heresy in policy and practice*, Springer Science, Dordrecht, The Netherlands.

Purcell-Gates V (2013) 'Literacy worlds of children of migrant farmworker communities participating in a Migrant Head Start Program', *Research in the Teaching of English*, 48(1):68–97.

Purcell-Gates V, Perry KH and Briseño A (2011) 'Analyzing literacy practice: grounded theory to model', *Research in the Teaching of English*, 45(4):439–458.

Rothery J (1990) *Story writing in the primary school: assessing narrative type genres* [unpublished PhD thesis], University of Sydney.

Rothery J (1996) 'Making changes: developing an educational linguistics', in Hasan R and Williams G (eds) *Literacy in society*, Longman, London.

Sahlberg P (2011) 'Paradoxes of educational improvement: the Finnish experience', *Scottish Educational Review*, 43(1):3–12.

Schwandt TA, Lincoln YS and Guba EG (2007) 'Judging interpretations: but is it rigorous? trustworthiness and authenticity in naturalistic evaluation', *New Directions for Evaluation*, 11–25.

Shanahan C and Shanahan T (2014) 'Does disciplinary literacy have a place in elementary school?', *The Reading Teacher*, 67(8):636–639.

Snow CE, Burns MS and Griffin P (eds) (1998) *Preventing reading difficulties in young children*, National Academy Press, Washington, DC.

Taber KS (2013) *Classroom-based research and evidence-based practice* (2nd edition), Sage, London.

The Design-based Research Collective (2003) 'Design-based research: an emerging paradigm for educational inquiry', *Educational Research*, 32(1):5–8.

Wu M (2016) 'What national testing can tell us', in Lingard B, Thompson G, and Sellar S (eds) *National testing in schools: an Australian assessment*, Routledge, London and New York.

Wyatt-Smith C, Elkins J and Gunn S (eds) (2011) *Multiple perspectives on difficulties in learning literacy and numeracy*, Springer International, Dordrecht, The Netherlands.

Wyatt-Smith C and Gunn S (2007) *Evidence-based research for expert literacy teaching*, Paper No. 12 (October 2007), Department of Education and Early Childhood Development, Melbourne.

Wyn J, Turnbull M and Grimshaw J (2014) *The experience of education: the impacts of high stakes testing on school students and their families — a qualitative study*, The Whitlam Institute, University of Western Sydney.

Xue Y and Meisels SJ (2004) 'Early literacy instruction and learning in kindergarten: evidence from the early childhood longitudinal study – kindergarten class of 1998–1999', *American Educational Research Journal*, 41(1):191–229.

Yin RK (2014) *Case study research: design and methods* (5th edition), Sage, Thousand Oaks, CA.

Young KA (2005) 'Direct from the source: the value of "think aloud" data in understanding learning', *Journal of Educational Enquiry*, 6(1):19–33.

CHAPTER 2

Oral language

Introduction

Literacy has been said 'to float on a sea of talk' (Britton 1970: 164). There is no doubt that children's oral language development precedes any kind of literate experiences and that young children demonstrate an innate desire to make meaning through language from the earliest stages of their development. Babies strive to make themselves heard and engage in interaction with others before their ability to use language develops. This can involve babbling and gurgling together with the use of volume and tone to get their needs met. This chapter will review the literature on the role of oral language in literacy learning and teaching by citing evidence-based research conducted in schools and suggesting programs and practices to support school leaders.

How oral language development can support achievement in literacy

Research in early years development identifies that oracy (Wilkinson 1970: 1), or oral language, is central to life and learning and that children's home language provides a rich resource to build on when the learner comes into the more formal years of schooling. Locke et al. (2002: 8) found in a large study in Sheffield, UK, with children aged between 3 and 7 years from identified low socioeconomic status (SES) backgrounds, that these children's mean results for receptive and expressive language were lower than average, falling 'on the boundary between normal and delayed language', with boys performing significantly lower than girls. However, general cognitive abilities were found to fall within the average range. Of interest here, is that language ability or oracy can mask cognitive abilities, and the recurrent theme of boy's language being often seen as delayed in the early years of schooling.

In a vastly multicultural and multilingual society such as Australia, we find this context further complicated by the enormous range of languages spoken at home and in families. It has been estimated that upwards of 21% of the population speaks a language other than English at home (ABS 2016).

In a high-stakes accountability school system, which focuses on outcomes in reading, writing, language conventions and spelling, spoken language might attract less attention than those traditional literate measures. But as we know, without oral language as a basis for making meaning, outcomes on literacy will be limited. The Australian Curriculum (ACARA 2014) promotes the development of oral language ability and knowledge in the early years of schooling; in fact, the Foundation Year content descriptors provide a strong platform for this work:

> ❯ ACELA1426: Understand that English is one of many languages spoken in Australia and that different languages may be spoken by family, classmates and community.
>
> ❯ ACELA1428: Explore how language is used differently at home and school depending on the relationships between people.
>
> ❯ ACELA1429: Understand that language can be used to explore ways of expressing needs, likes and dislikes.

A further factor that underpins the centrality of oracy in the beginnings of becoming literate is for young children to have a sophisticated understanding of the differences between the way that oral language is structured, and the way written language is structured. Teachers often talk about this difference during modelled reading or guided reading, and research tells us that this simple understanding can support confident movement into becoming a reader and a writer (Skidmore et al. 2003).

High-quality talk about language is important in fostering students' understanding of the language choices they make when they are writing and speaking (Myhill 2016; Myhill et al. 2020), including seeing the relationships and differences between written and spoken language. Research by Pianta and Stuhlman (2004) extends this idea by aligning processes in literacy development with specific roles for teachers. They identify 2 key starting points. The first is the recognition that the skills processes that begin in infancy are essential to later literacy behavioural processes. The second is the teacher–child interactions that take place around literacy-related skills and processes (such as sensitive stimulation of oral language). These interactions also support other development outcomes, such as social competence and self-regulation, which in turn support literacy development.

Pianta (2006) goes on to emphasise that when early interactions with print in social and meaningful ways are foregrounded while also teaching elements of early reading skills through oral language, the chances of developing successful readers are higher. Pianta suggests that this oral language focus is also useful as reading skills grow beyond the foundation years and that the continual foregrounding of talk about reading with the teacher develops strong readers in later primary years. Thus, teacher–child relationships and the importance of a focus on oral language to mediate this in the classrooms are important in that they have both social and instructional dimensions.

Work from the United Kingdom by Alexander (2008) argues that across school years, spoken language should have the same status as written language, because it is fundamental to thinking and learning, as well as to communication. In fact, Vygotsky (1978) says that the fundamental role of social interaction is the development of cognition, as he believed strongly that community plays a central role in the process of making meaning.

Vygotsky (1962) also tells us that thought and language are initially separate systems, and at the age of around 3 years, speech and thought become interdependent. By this, he means that thought becomes verbal and speech becomes representational. These internal verbal monologues that thus become inner speech are central to the development of cognition during the early school years.

> *Inner speech is not the interior aspect of external speech – it is a function in itself. It still remains speech, i.e., thought connected with words. But while in external speech thought is embodied in words, in inner speech words die as they bring forth thought. Inner speech is to a large extent thinking in pure meanings. (Vygotsky 1962 :149)*

Inner speech continues throughout the school years and beyond, and most importantly this inner speech accompanies a learner into their early encounters with books, explicit aspects of print and early reading. The role of the teacher in co-constructing and developing internalisation of language is important as it drives cognitive development and provides support for the strong link between talk and thought.

In summary, the importance of oral language development, classroom talk, and oracy cannot be underestimated in relation to the movement to becoming literate in the early years classroom. If children do not have experience of oracy as a mode of learning and a means of expression, then there is a risk that their cognitive, personal, relationship and emotional development may be restricted. This is particularly relevant for boys' learning (Younger et al. 2005).

Strategies to help literacy achievement in your school

The opening section of this chapter has focused specifically on the alignment of oral language development and early literacy skills. For school leaders, it is important that early years teachers value the essential place of talk for social interactive reasons in the classroom and understand how the explicit teaching of early literacy skills and knowledge can support all learners in their classrooms.

Elements of a rich oracy curriculum according to Bearne and Reedy (2018) are listed below. They say that classrooms displaying these types of activities are providing opportunities for learners to hear and use oral language to enhance their learning of literacy. Students need to:

- hear good models of spoken language
- speak audibly and fluently
- listen and respond appropriately, adapting spoken language to a wide range of contexts
- explore and discuss features of spoken language; distinguish between formal and informal types of spoken language and know when it is appropriate to use each
- participate actively in collaborative conversations, in groups and class and use the conventions of group discussion
- ask relevant questions to extend understanding to seek information, views and feelings and build a spoken language repertoire
- speculate, hypothesise and explore ideas
- give extended spoken responses to questions, books, poems and visual texts
- articulate and justify answers, arguments and opinions
- give clear descriptions and explanations
- listen and respond to a range of fiction, poetry, drama and media texts through the use of traditional and digital resources
- explore the richness and diversity of language and its personal and creative purposes
- reflect on and explain their literacy and thinking skills, using feedback to refine ideas and sensitively provide useful feedback for others

> engage in a range of imaginative and creative spoken language, for example, drama, role play, storytelling, poetry, presentations, performances and debates. (Bearne and Reedy 2018)

As learners move through the early literacy stage and become more confident, oral language can help them understand the curriculum content and can be used to interact and to express ideas. The Australian Curriculum: English (AC:E) provides us with clear directions around the place of oral language in the English curriculum and it shows a clear progression from early years to the later years of schooling. In particular, the sub-strands below demonstrate how strongly the AC:E can support cross-school planning for oral language use.

Table 2.1. The place of oral language in the Australian Curriculum: English

	STRAND		
	Language	**Literature**	**Literacy**
Description	In the language strand, students develop their knowledge of the English language and how it works.	The literature strand aims to build students' knowledge about how language can be used for aesthetic ends, to create particular emotional, intellectual or philosophical effects.	The literacy strand aims to develop students' ability to interpret and create texts with appropriateness, accuracy, confidence, fluency and efficacy.
Sub-strand	Language for interaction	Responding to literature	Interacting with others
Threads	Language for social interactions	Personal responses to the ideas, characters and viewpoints in texts	Listening and speaking interactions (purposes and contexts)
	Evaluative language	Expressing preferences and evaluating texts	Listening and speaking interactions (skills)
			Oral presentations

If a school adopts an explicit oral language or talk policy across their school grades and aligns these with national, state or jurisdictional curriculum documents, and school scope and sequence charts bringing in the cross-curriculum perspectives, the school is recognising that spoken language is the foundation of children's personal, social, cultural, cognitive, creative and imaginative development. Oral language can provide the means of thinking through ideas as well as a medium of communication. It will also underpin literacy learning as the demands of comprehending and composing texts increase across the years of schooling.

CLASSROOM TALK

As learners move through the schooling process, spoken language is not only the basis of reading and writing but has a repertoire of its own that deserves equal attention in teaching. Classroom talk has gained focus in recent years as the makeup of school populations becomes more diverse and as so much of the pedagogical leadership coming from systems and school leaders becomes aware of the importance of constructivist curriculum 'floating on a sea of talk'.

Gibbons (2006: 114–117) categorises different types of classroom talk according to students' participation (ranging from least to greatest participation), namely, 'teacher monologue', 'IRF' (Initiation-Response-Feedback), 'dialogic exchanges' and 'participatory exchanges'.

Figure 2.1 shows these types of classroom talk defined and placed on a continuum, from teacher controlled to student controlled.

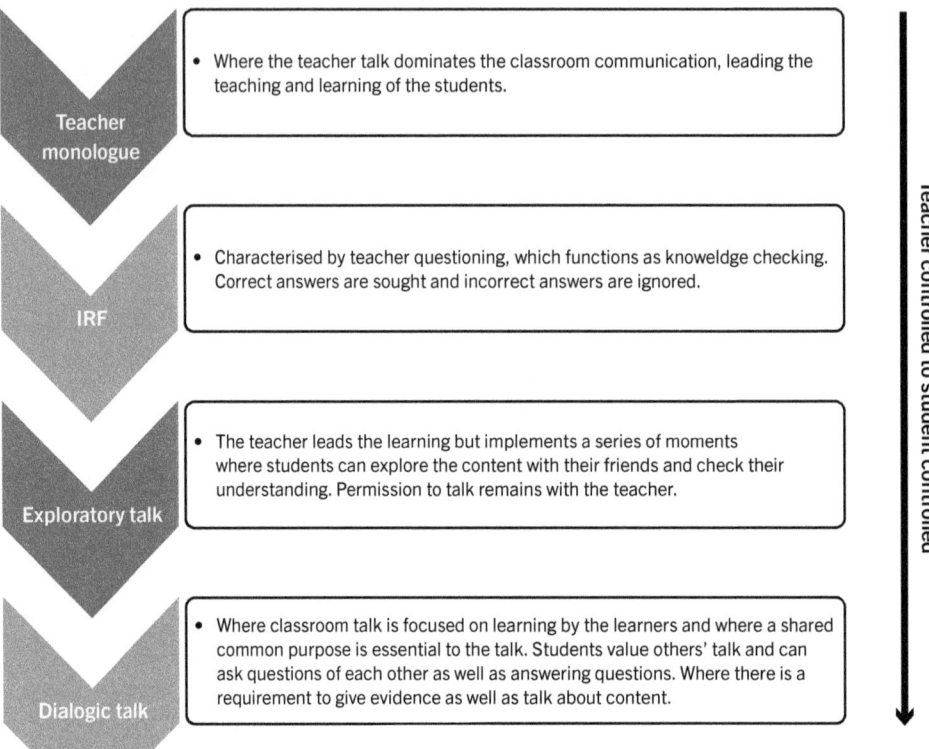

Figure 2.1. Continuum of classroom talk

Teacher monologue

Teacher monologue (Wells 2001) refers to the teacher talking to the learners in a singular direction, where knowledge and content flows from the teacher into the 'empty vessels' in front of the teacher. Students are to listen and understand and the learning is seen as the responsibility of the student alone. At times, the students ask questions, but it is expected that these will be about fine tuning the information delivered by the teacher. A further use of teacher monologue is a form of behaviour management, where when the teacher is speaking, the students are silent.

IRF (initiation–response–feedback)

In this form of classroom talk, the teacher uses a so-called 'discourse move' to provide input for students, as in teacher monologue, but incorporating a questioning process to check understanding. Research tells us that this is common in English classrooms and across the curriculum and Cazden (1988) identified this as a default position because she found that many teachers returned to it. The classroom IRF (sometimes known as IRE) has been researched by many of those interested in classroom talk (Wells 1999; Mercer 1995; Baker and Freebody 1989; Alexander 2001) and it has become the springboard for other researchers to consider other classroom discourses that might be more effective.

Exploratory talk

Douglas Barnes (1976) provides one of the first platforms for acknowledging the importance of talk in classrooms; his work falls mainly under the heading of 'exploratory talk'. Barnes explains this as talk between learners that moves thinking forward and allows for the exploration of ideas and the forming of new conceptualisations of information and knowledge. Exploratory talk by learners is identified as being hesitant and incomplete. In classrooms, learners can talk together and confirm their understandings of the content the teachers are introducing. However, exploratory talk still maintains the 'status quo' of teacher as leader of the talk and controller of when and how to talk about the content. Common classroom examples of exploratory talk are talking partners, think-pair-share, group work, joint construction of texts, and shoulder talk.

Dialogic talk

In contrast to the forms of classroom talk above, dialogic talk requires teachers and students to engage in a genuine dialogue to take part together in a process of genuine enquiry. The work of Alexander (2001, 2008) develops and discusses a way of looking at talk in classrooms that moves beyond answering questions and exploring ideas to creating new knowledge and becoming active meaning makers who progress through talk and interaction to higher levels of cognitive development.

According to Alexander (2008), dialogic discussion involves learners collectively formulating, defending and examining others' viewpoints and eventually constructing new understandings.

Dialogic teaching is different to exploratory talk, IRF and monologic talk in ways suggested by Reznitskaya (2012) when she writes about the big picture of teaching and learning. In dialogic teaching, 'the purpose of schooling shifts from the acquisition of established facts to the internalization of intellectual competencies that underlie the development of disciplinary knowledge' (Reznitskaya 2012: 448).

All of this discussion around types of classroom talk underscores the importance of careful planning for talk in the classroom, for supporting learning and the development of individual and higher order thinking skills. However, the literature warns to not adhere strongly to any particular type of talk (as described in Figure 2.1). Instead, it points to the efficacy of linking a dialogic talk-based classroom discourse with the development of student higher order thinking (Nystrand et al. 2003; Wegerif et al. 1999). Dialogic talk builds higher order thinking skills and supports the reader in moving into using reading strategies in upper primary years, where synthesis and analysis are essential for completing reading tasks. Dialogic talk is thus placed as an essential element as learners move to upper primary and early secondary classrooms and prepare for the reading demands of the curriculum at these stages.

Further classroom talk strategies

Lawrence and Snow (2016) in the *Handbook of reading research* state that '[r]esearch strongly supports the claim that when students have extended time for engaged conversation about text, they are likely to comprehend what they read better, and to build autonomous comprehension and writing skills.' Extended time allocation and deeper conversation about text builds rich discussions in the classroom. In a similar way to dialogic teaching, both teachers and students have authority and participation rights in the discussion, the questions are meaningful and worth discussion and an end goal for the discussion is clear to all involved. Central to this is that time is allocated within the teacher's planning together with the rules for interaction – this may include:

building on an earlier contribution; raising a further question to take the dialogue forward; and ensuring all have a chance to speak.

Figure 2.2 looks at classroom talk from where the teacher is placed and how the talk might be configured within the classroom interaction. If the figure is read from the top to the bottom, we can see how the teacher's role in leading the talk diminishes, thus handing the talk to the students. When purposeful and exploratory student talk dominates the classroom talk, real learning takes place, as students are required to think, hypothesise and test out their ideas through talk.

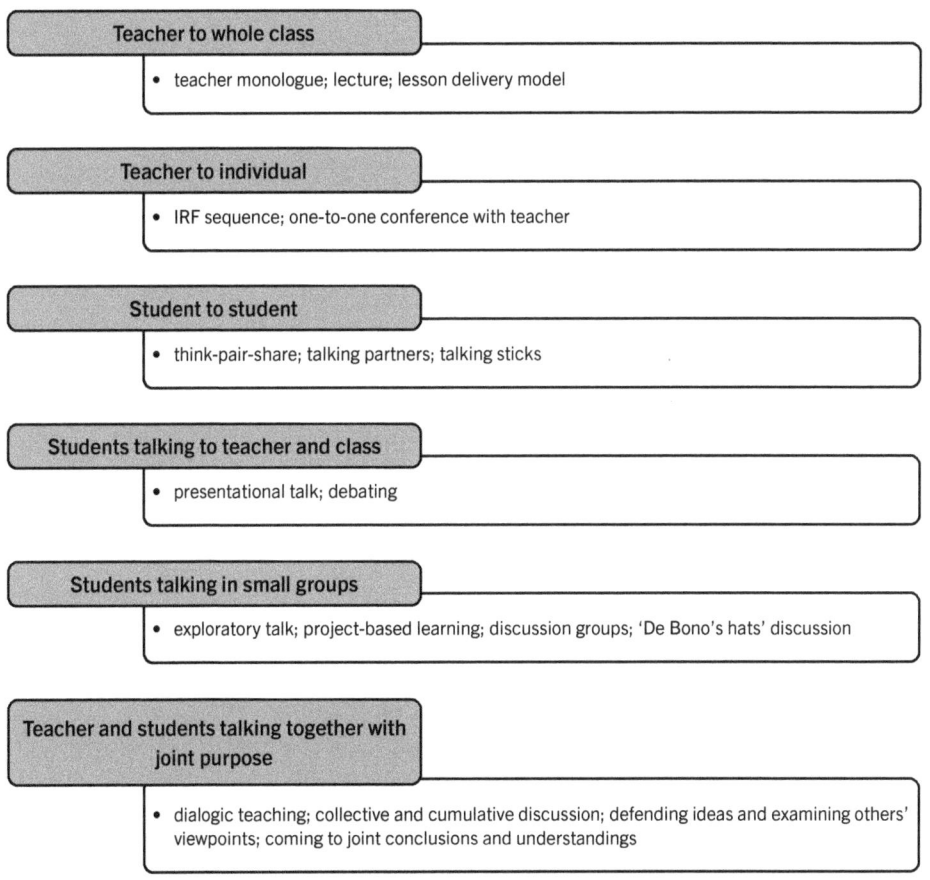

Figure 2.2. Teacher talk and classroom strategies for oral language development

MAXIMISING TALK WITH LANGUAGE BACKGROUND OTHER THAN ENGLISH (LBOTE) LEARNERS

Any good oral language program facilitates English language acquisition with those for whom English is not their main language and those who speak a dialect that may not be the same as the dialect of English used in their classroom (Delpit 2006; Heath 1983). However, research and practice in teaching English to learners tells us repeatedly that there needs to be a more explicit and tailored focus for English language learners who are learning in and through English as a second language. The seminal work of Cummins (1999, 2003, 2008) demonstrates one of the most important aspects of this difference between 'language 1' classroom learners and 'language 2' classroom learners.

Cummins (1999) identified 'basic interpersonal communicative skills' (BICS), which describes the development of conversational fluency in the second language, whereas 'cognitive academic language proficiency' (CALP) describes the use of language in decontextualised academic situations. The importance of this distinction is that at times English as a second language learners appear to have learnt English because they are able to demonstrate BICS after one or 2 years in school, whereas CALP may take upwards of 7 years to fully operate in a decontextualised academic situation in a classroom. This clearly has serious implications for LBOTE students in our schools.

The research tells us that the solution to this situation is to continue students' cognitive academic language and knowledge in their own language while learning English as a second language – this, of course, describes bilingual education.

The research is very clear about the importance of bilingual children's mother tongue for their overall personal and educational development. Summarised below are the findings of more than 135 research studies, most notably found in the work of Gersten and Baker (2000), Cummins (2003), and Skutnabb-Kangas (2006).

> Bilingualism has positive effects on children's linguistic and educational development.

> The level of development of children's mother tongue is a strong predictor of their second language development.

> Mother tongue promotion in the school helps develop not only the mother tongue but also children's abilities in the majority school language.

> Spending instructional time through a minority language in the school does not hurt children's academic development in the majority school language.

> Children's mother tongues are fragile and easily lost in the early years of school.

> To reject a child's language in the school is to reject the child.

Educational policy in Australia does not support bilingual education and since the early part of the twenty-first century, many aspects of financial support for multilingual learners and LBOTE students have been included under the larger support arrangements for literacy. Having said that, many jurisdictions and school systems operate strong evidence-based practices for these students through government or non-government bilingual programs operating in some schools. School leaders will find that staff who work with these students in their schools will be aware of the work summarised in this section of the chapter.

Reflections from school leaders

This response comes from Helen West. Helen has been a primary school teacher in Inner West Sydney for decades and has provided system leadership to Sydney Catholic Schools in English as an Additional Language or Dialect (EAL/D) and early literacy. Her leadership in this area has influenced school leaders in making sure that oral language development is central to their approach to school literacy programs. Further to this, Helen's work at school level has supported many hundreds of teachers in making oral language central to literacy learning.

Question 1: What does a school-based approach to an explicit oral language program look like?

The curriculum is a rich resource for the development of an explicit and well-planned oral language program. It can serve 2 purposes: scaffolding the development of the academic language required for reading and writing in different subject areas, and [functioning] as a cognitive tool, playing an important role in student learning (Vygotsky 1962), for example, the ability to question and critique ideas.

One approach is for oral language programs to have a communicative purpose, where students work in pairs/small groups with a focus on speaking and listening. It requires students to practice using the new academic language in context of the topic/subject area to complete the task. The task has an 'information gap' where all students do not have the same information, so they must share their information to complete the task – e.g. think-pair-share; jigsaw reading; dictogloss; cloze; split dictation. Such activities allow students to focus on how language makes meaning, which is essential for the reading and writing process.

Question 2: Do you think that a whole school focus on oral language contributes to raising student achievement?

The Australian Curriculum identifies listening and speaking as important skills, along with reading, viewing and writing, in being literate in today's society. The ability to use oral language to both comprehend and compose texts across different subject areas is crucial. For students to be able to 'talk their way in' to challenging concepts and abstract ideas in any subject area and use this new knowledge to respond to and show their understanding through reading and writing, is necessary in becoming literate.

For teachers too, they have an important role in making student–teacher talk (and listening) more 'learning rich' for students. [This might range] through extending teacher–student exchanges and probing student responses to designing collaborative tasks that provide opportunities for meaningful oral interactions in different subject areas. Importantly, teachers need to talk about how language works – metalanguage – and draw student attention to the difference between spoken language and written language when composing and responding to a diverse range of texts.

School-wide improvement

Lawrence and Snow (2016) point out that when a school system has a focus on accountability and easily tested skills, this can reduce teachers' willingness to invest time in classroom discussion and that there is a need for more robust evidence to demonstrate improvements in reading comprehension and writing gains. They make a stronger point that development of oral language skills across a system or at a school policy level should be seen as an end in itself rather than as a means to improve easily testable literacy outcomes. I would go even further to suggest that what is outlined in this chapter is a 'long game' for a school leader to take part in, and that school improvement will follow when teachers and students are involved in a rich talk curriculum. As Lawrence and Snow (2016) indicate, the research supports the claim that a rich oral language curriculum results in gains in literacy.

School leaders can also undertake ongoing professional discussions with classroom teachers, instructional leaders and learning support teachers. Basing these discussions about how a school-wide talk curriculum can support literacy learning on the topics of collective and cumulative discussion, examining others' viewpoints, defending ideas and coming to joint conclusions and understandings will all prove useful.

Annotated bibliography

Cameron S and Dempsey L (2016) *The oral language book*, S & L Publishing, Auckland, New Zealand.

>This book includes foundational theory for the role of oral language in classrooms, with chapters on vocabulary development, drama, presentations, listening and planning for a speaking and listening classroom. It provides lessons ideas and photocopiable resources.

Edwards-Groves C, Anstey M and Bull G (2014) *Classroom talk: understanding dialogue, pedagogy and practice*, Primary English Teaching Association of Australia, Newtown, NSW.

>This book builds a strong theoretical basis for making classrooms more explicitly social learning places. It gives very specific lessons around exploring texts through talk and uses the Australian Curriculum: English as its basis.

Jones P, Simpson, A and Thwaite A (2018) (eds) *Talking the talk: snapshots from Australian classrooms*, Primary English Teaching Association of Australia, Newtown, NSW.

>This book provides detailed classroom examples of how classrooms can support learners' capacity to use talk to think, to speculate, to hypothesise, to dream.

Parkin B and Harper H (2018) *Teaching with intent: scaffolding academic language with marginalised students*, Primary English Teaching Association of Australia, Newtown, NSW.

>This book provides an in-depth overview of how to use oral language in classrooms to scaffold learning. It provides micro-scaffolding techniques where a focus text is used to assist students to work from oral language to written language in science.

Parkin B and Harper H (2019) *Teaching with intent 2: literature-based literacy teaching and learning*, Primary English Teaching Association of Australia, Newtown, NSW.

>A second book building on the micro-scaffold introduced in their earlier book, this title focuses on literature and creates possibilities for students to make sense of new language through purposeful classroom dialogue.

REFERENCES

ABS (Australian Bureau of Statistics) (2012) *2011 Census QuickStats*, ABS website, accessed 3 March 2022. https://quickstats.censusdata.abs.gov.au/census_services/getproduct/census/2011/quickstat/0

ACARA (Australian Curriculum, Assessment and Reporting Authority) (2014) F–10 curriculum, English, Key ideas, ACARA website, accessed 8 March 2022. https://www.australiancurriculum.edu.au/f-10-curriculum/english/key-ideas/

Alexander R (2001) *Culture and pedagogy: international comparisons in primary education*, Blackwell, Oxford.

Alexander R (2008) *Towards dialogic teaching: rethinking classroom talk*, Dialogos, Cambridge.

Baker C and Freebody P (1985) *Children's first school books*, Oxford, Blackwell.

Barnes D (1976) *From communication to curriculum in the secondary classroom*, Penguin, Hammondsworth.

Beard R (2000) *Developing Writing 3–13*, Hodder & Stoughton, London.

Bearne E and Reedy D (2018) *Teaching primary English: subject knowledge and classroom practice*, Routledge, Abingdon.

Cameron S and Dempsey L (2016) *The oral language book*, S & L Publishing, Auckland, New Zealand.

Cazden CB (1988) *Classroom discourse: the language of teaching and learning*, Heinemann, Portsmouth, NH.

Cummins J (1999) *BICS and CALP: clarifying the distinction* (Report No. ED438551), ERIC Clearinghouse on Languages and Linguistics, Washington, DC.

Cummins J (2003) *Bilingual education: basic principles*, Multilingual Matters, Bristol.

Cummins J (2008) 'BICS and CALP: empirical and theoretical status of the distinction', *Encyclopedia of Language and Education*, 2(2):71–83.

Delpit L (2006) *Other people's children: cultural conflict in the classroom*, The New Press, New York.

Edwards-Groves C, Anstey M and Bull G (2014) *Classroom talk: understanding dialogue, pedagogy and practice*, Primary English Teaching Association of Australia, Newtown, NSW.

Gersten R and Baker S (2000) 'What we know about effective instructional practices for English-language learners', *Exceptional Children*, 66(4), 454–470.

Gibbons P (2006) *Bridging discourses in the ESL classroom: students, teachers and researchers*, Bloomsbury Academic, London.

Heath SB (1983) *Ways with words: language, life and work in communities and classrooms*, Cambridge University Press, Cambridge.

Jones P, Simpson, A and Thwaite A (2018) (eds) *Talking the talk: snapshots from Australian classrooms*, Primary English Teaching Association of Australia, Newtown, NSW.

Lawrence JF and Snow CE (2016) 'Oral discourse and reading', in Barr R, Kamil ML, Mosenthal PB and Pearson DP (2016) *Handbook of reading research*, Routledge.

Locke A, Ginsborg J and Peers I (2002) 'Development and disadvantage: implications for the early years and beyond', *International Journal of Language and Communication Disorders*, 37:3–16.

Mercer N (1995) *The guided construction of knowledge: how we use language to think together*, Multilingual Matters, Clevedon.

Myhill DA and Newman R (2016) 'Metatalk: enabling metalinguistic discussion about writing', *International Journal of Education Research*, 80:177–187.

Myhill D, Newman R and Watson A (2020) 'Going meta: dialogic talk in the writing classroom', *Australian Journal of Language and Literacy,* 43(1), 5–16.

Nystrand M, Wu L, Gamoran A, Zeiser S and Long DA (2003) 'Questions in time: investigating the structure and dynamics of unfolding classroom discourse', *Discourse Processes*, 35(2):135–198.

Parkin B and Harper H (2018) *Teaching with intent: scaffolding academic language with marginalised students*, Primary English Teaching Association of Australia, Newtown, NSW.

Parkin B and Harper H (2019) *Teaching with intent 2: literature-based literacy teaching and learning*, Primary English Teaching Association of Australia, Newtown, NSW.

Pianta RC (2006) 'Teacher–child relationships and early literacy', *Handbook of Early Literacy Research*, 2:149–162.

Pianta RC and Stuhlman MW (2004) 'Teacher–child relationships and children's success in the first years of school', *School Psychology Review*, 33:444–458.

Reznitskaya A (2012) 'Dialogic teaching: rethinking language use during literature discussions', *The Reading Teacher*, 65(7):446–456.

Skidmore D, Perez-Parent M and Arnfield S (2003) 'Teacher–pupil dialogue in the guided reading session', *Reading*, 37(2):47–53.

Skutnabb-Kangas T (2006) 'Language policy and linguistic human rights', in Ricento T (ed) *An introduction to language policy: theory and method*, Blackwell Publishing, Malden, MA.

Vygotsky LS (1962) 'Thought and word', in Vygotsky L, Hanfmann E, Vakar G (eds) *Thought and language*, MIT Press.

Vygotsky LS (1978) *Mind in society: the development of higher psychological processes*, Harvard University Press, Cambridge, MA.

Wegerif R, Mercer N and Dawes L (1999) 'From social interaction to individual reasoning: an empirical investigation of a possible sociocultural model of cognitive development', *Learning and Instruction*, 9(6):493–516.

Wells G (1999) *Dialogic enquiry: towards a socio-cultural practice and theory of education*, Cambridge University Press, Cambridge.

Wells G (ed) (2001) *Action, talk, and text: learning and teaching through inquiry* (Vol. 16), Teachers College Press.

Wilkinson A (1970) 'The concept of oracy', *The English Journal*, 59(1):71–77.

Younger M, Warrington M and McLellan R (2005) *Raising boys' achievement in secondary schools: issues, dilemmas and opportunities*, McGraw-Hill Education (UK).

CHAPTER 3

Teaching grammar and writing

Introduction

The English language is complex and, for the majority of young learners, opaque – many young English mother tongue speakers and second or other language speakers have mastered the use of oral language but are unable to reflect on or consider the rules of language in use. Interestingly, those who speak English as a second or other language often have greater insight into the structure of English. This chapter will outline the research evidence around the teaching of knowledge about the English language and how it functions and is structured. It will also discuss how an understanding of the grammar of the English language can enhance students' use of and understanding of English, particularly for the purpose of reading and writing.

THE HISTORY OF GRAMMAR TEACHING

The development of ways of describing the English language and how it works has an interesting history and for the purpose of school leadership, is worthwhile to consider at the beginning of this chapter. English was an oral language for much of its development and it was not until ecclesiastical scholars and scribes in the Middle Ages began to write in English rather than Latin that it was recorded. Teachers and scholars of the English language overlaid Latin grammar in the analysis and teaching of English until the early 1900s, when grammarians began to look at the structures and functions of English grammar in its own right.

An historic look at the ways in which grammar has been presented in school classrooms over the last 150 years provides a logical place to start. Figure 3.1 summarises how we have thought about grammar in the last 100 years and provides an initial mapping of the field. Following this overview, the chapter will explore recent research that indicates how the explicit teaching of grammar has raised student outcomes in writing tasks.

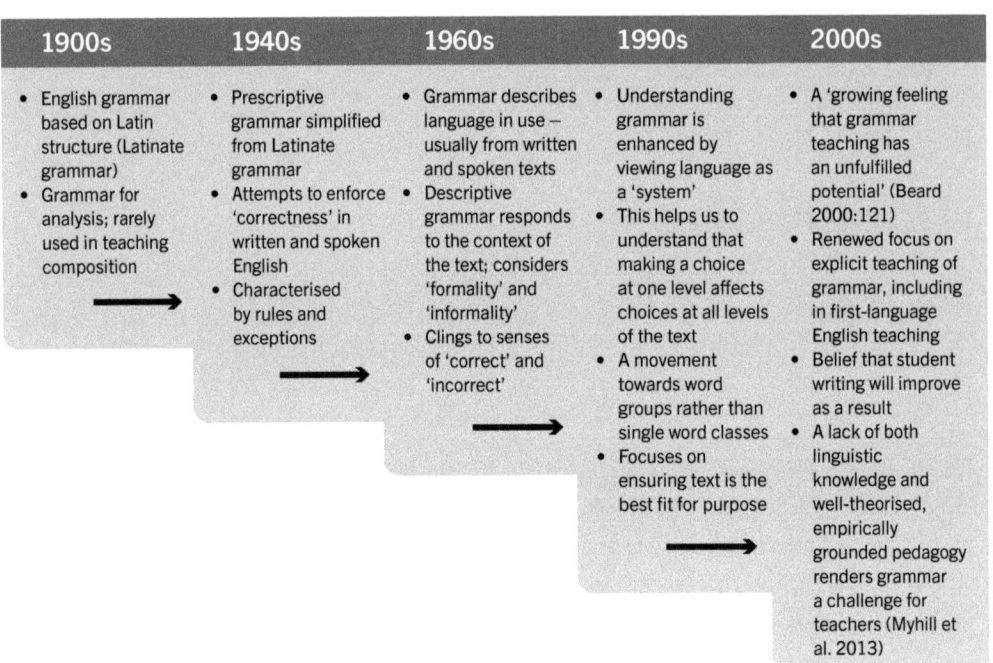

Figure 3.1. 100 years of grammar in schools and society

The teaching of grammar for much of the last 100 years was characterised by didactic pedagogy, where teachers taught abstract concepts to young learners who may have struggled with the need to reflect on language and how it works. Interestingly, the Grammar School system from the United Kingdom is so called because it originally taught Latinate grammar and was known for selective admissions and a more academic curriculum than the modern 'comprehensive schools'.

In the 1950s, linguistics as a field of study sharpened its focus on the grammar of the English language, looking in particular at language in use. Linguists asked questions like, 'How does the structure of oral language indicate number or tense?' Such questions are about language in use rather than applying known rules to language, and thus are examples of descriptive rather than prescriptive linguistics. Educational linguists became involved in developing materials for schools and teaching and learning contexts where the focus was more on 'Is the utterance meaningful?' and 'Can the language users understand each other?' However, to this day, the use of prescriptive linguistics or traditional grammar remains in schools and systems, most notably in books and worksheets used to teach the correct use of grammar, where learners fill in the correct pronoun or verb.

An example is:

Choose the correct form of the verb in the following sentence:

The children (**went/go**) to the beach yesterday.

An example from the NAPLAN language conventions sample test paper demonstrates this further:

Which words complete the second sentence:

The children went to the pool yesterday. Some of them _____ again today but it was closed.

> was planning to go
> were planning to go
> is planning to go
> are planning to go

More recently, the work of functional linguistics has made an impact on the teaching of grammar in schools. Functional linguists consider that meaning is central to language use and that the language user (whether it be oral language or written language) makes a series of choices about which words they use and that these choices are remarkably similar.

How explicit teaching of grammar can support achievement in literacy and writing

EVIDENCE FOR EXPLICIT TEACHING OF GRAMMAR

Research evidence abounds for the explicit teaching of grammar or a metalanguage to school-aged learners and the following section will explore this. The findings and effects sizes will be presented from 2 meta-analyses, one with adolescent learners (Graham and Perin 2007) and one in the early grades (Koster et al. 2015), followed by findings from other more qualitative research.

Meta-analyses

The primary purpose of the Graham and Perin (2007) review was to identify effective practices for teaching writing to adolescents (Grades 4 to 12 in the US). This analysis was based on quantitative studies that had an intervention in one group and that was compared to a different intervention or no intervention in another. The analyses were conducted on the basis that instructional approaches can have a broad impact on writing performance. A meta-analysis seeks to find which intervention has the most powerful effect, known as the effect size. It summarises the effect through a set of findings from quantitative studies measuring the magnitude of the success of the experiment. Thus, the larger the effect size, the stronger the relationship between 2 variables.

At a general level, the findings showed that explicitly and systematically teaching the processes and strategies involved in writing (including planning, sentence construction, summarising and revising) raises writing outcomes. The findings also placed the teacher in a structured and instructional role requiring the teacher to provide a model example of the final text, thus providing very clear writer goals. Graham and Perin (2007) observed that there were 6 adolescent writing teaching strategies in their meta-analysis that had effect sizes larger than 0.5 (high effect size and strong relationship with the instructional variable). These are strategies that teach students how to:

> plan, revise and edit their writing
> summarise reading material prior to writing
> work together to plan, draft, revise and edit their writing
> identify and set specific goals and purposes for the writing
> use a word processor as a primary tool for writing
> write increasingly more complex sentences and combine simple sentences into more sophisticated ones.

Other positive effect sizes pointed to teacher professional learning, inquiry-based instructions, and providing good models of writing as the focus of the instruction.

So, where is the explicit instruction in grammar in this meta-analysis? Graham and Perin (2007) found only one variable that had a negative effect size. This was the teaching of grammar (an effect size of -0.32). The authors suggest caution is needed in interpreting this finding as there was only one study in the 123 in the meta-analysis where grammar instruction was the control condition. This is the study by Fearn and Farnan (2005), who found that teaching students to focus on the function and practical application of grammar within the context of writing (versus defining and describing grammar) produced strong and positive effects on students' writing.

A further meta-analysis (Koster et al. 2015) sought to answer the question: Which instructional practices effectively improve the writing performance of students in the upper elementary grades? The meta-analysis was conducted using 37 studies focused on upper primary grades of Year 4 to Year 7. Once again, a negative effect size was found for grammar instruction, and it was concluded that this did not improve the quality of students' writing. So, what was effective? Interventions where effect size was significantly higher than zero were goal setting, strategy instruction, feedback, text structure instruction and peer assistance. When further statistical analysis was done, it was found that goal setting was by far the most effective intervention, with feedback also proving to be effective, however, not more effective than prewriting activities.

What then of the role of grammar instruction as a high-impact practice in producing improved writing outcomes? Each of the 3 main meta-analyses in the teaching of writing (Hillocks 1986; Graham and Perin 2007; Graham et al. 2012) found negative effects for grammar instruction in writing achievement. What we need to consider is the nature of the grammar instruction – the meta-analyses all suggest that when grammar is taught in isolation or as a set of knowledge outside a 'real' writing situation, it may not be clear to students how to apply what they have learnt when writing a text.

Qualitative research

We will now look at some smaller and more qualitative studies where grammar was taught in the context of 'real writing'. There have been a series of studies conducted by Myhill and her colleagues in the UK (Jones et al. 2013; Myhill, Jones, Watson 2013; Myhill, Jones, Watson, Lines 2013) where they consider the teaching of grammar within a 'real' writing situation, in part to address the consistent research findings that there are no strong effect sizes found between discrete grammar instruction and positive writing outcomes. Myhill (2010) has advocated that grammar is part of the teaching of writing and should focus on the communicative act of writing, which helps writers understand the social purposes of text and the importance of language use for meaning making. In a special issue of the *Journal of Research in Reading*, Myhill and Fisher (2010: 1) note that writing is:

> ❯ cognitively costly, requiring complex processing that places a high demand on working memory

> ❯ socio-culturally complex; writers must shape their writing to the needs of their readers

> linguistically complex; writers must navigate linguistic choices and make the correct choice each time.

Within the teaching of writing, grammar can be utilised as a resource for meaning. In response to calls for a study that tested whether teaching grammar as part of the teaching of writing was effective, Myhill et al. (2012) published the results of their study conducted in 32 Year 8 classrooms (*n=744*) in the UK where embedded grammar teaching intervention took place in half of the classrooms, while the remaining classrooms had no embedded grammar teaching. The embedded grammar teaching comprised detailed teaching schemes in which a meaningful connection could be made between the grammar point and the writing task.

Myhill et al. (2012) found that there were improvements for both groups, demonstrated through comparisons between the pre and post tests. However, the intervention group showed a more robust improvement – some 5 per cent higher than the control group. Of course, there were many more subtle measures than this, one of which showed that the intervention had a greater effect on the more able students. It is hypothesised that the more able students had a better understanding of how to incorporate the taught aspects of grammar into their writing. Other findings were drawn by Myhill and her team that connected teacher knowledge of grammar to the intervention outcomes, by including lesson observations and other qualitative measures. Myhill et al. (2012) claim that this is the first large-scale study in any country of the benefits or otherwise of teaching grammar within a purposeful context in writing.

A logical progression from this broad international review of research would be to consider research conducted in Australian classrooms. It is here that we need to pause. There is very little recent large-scale research that considers the relationship between the teaching of grammar and writing outcomes in Australian schools. It is true that the teaching of grammar in Australian schools has had a renewed focus and the 'Australian Curriculum: English' has drawn teachers and system and school leaders' attention to ways of thinking about grammar and ways of ensuring that it is in school planning documents. However, most of the research in the teaching of grammar in schools has come from the direction of teacher knowledge about language. My own study of the teaching of writing in upper primary school focused on teacher knowledge about language and found that this was usually based on teachers' own school experiences when being taught grammar (Cox 2001). This knowledge was based on descriptive grammars, such as word class, tense and number. Teachers also had little to draw on when teaching writing as they had not been provided with a sophisticated enough model of grammar during teacher education. The study focused on the ways in which teachers set out the purpose, audience and genre of the writing task in 10 upper primary classrooms but did not look at learner writing outcomes.

Other well-known Australian studies since have also focused more on teacher knowledge of grammar and how this shapes the pedagogy in their writing classrooms. For example, Macken-Horarik et al. (2011, 2015) worked primarily with teachers in improving and fine tuning their knowledge about language and having them use this in planning for teaching writing. Teachers in these studies did teach writing lessons and reported on the success of the lessons, but no clear connection to student outcomes were made.

Another recent study by Jones and Chen (2012) similarly conducted a knowledge audit of 53 teachers in one primary and one secondary school in NSW. The 3-phase study initially saw these teachers complete a 'knowledge about language' survey. The second phase was an intervention where 15 teachers took part in grammar knowledge workshops based on the model of language in the Australian Curriculum: English. The third phase followed 5 of these teachers into the classroom to observe their teaching of grammar before and after the intervention workshops. The study clearly identifies the strong need for teachers to be supported in the teaching of grammar in classrooms, both from a knowledge base and a pedagogical base. Once again, no connection with learner outcomes in writing was made in this study.

Other researchers have focused on the knowledge about language of pre-service teachers. A study by Harper and Rennie (2009) surveyed pre-service teachers about their grammatical knowledge, based on their reading of 3 short texts and their ability to talk about the letters, syllables and sounds, sentence structure and genre as well as a series of other items in the instrument. The researchers concluded that the pre-service teachers lacked analytical ability to discuss how language works and called on pre-service teacher education programs to actively build the students' knowledge about language, not just in a didactic manner but through conversations about text.

One case study by Humphrey and Macnaught (2015) does something a little more than the previously cited studies; it explores how teachers teach students whose language background is not English to write a grammatically correct piece. The study is situated in a single secondary school where 97 per cent of the students have a language background other than English and have poor results in NAPLAN writing scores, and fail to improve in secondary school. Teachers at the school are also often at a loss as to how to build grammatical knowledge to improve written texts. This study goes some way to taking the next step of identifying teachers' lack of grammatical knowledge, building that knowledge and linking this intervention to the student writing outcomes.

Humphrey and Macnaught's (2015) study was conducted over a 2-year period with one teacher and her Year 7 to 8 English class. The data was derived from a corpus of student texts (*n=178*) collected over an 18-month period. Concurrently, 6 audio transcripts of recorded classroom and lesson dialogues were collected. These transcripts showed that in the early lessons in the study, teachers were focusing on the concepts of the lesson, with no links to how a written text might demonstrate this conceptual knowledge. So, writers struggled to complete the tasks set. Later on in the study, analysis of classroom talk in English has evidence of explicit instruction in modelling exemplar texts and the substantial use of metalanguage by the teacher and by the students in responding to other students' writing. The study showed that the explicit scaffolding and use of the metalanguage from the intervention facilitated the teacher's ability to support the student writers. The positive findings from the study were demonstrated through growth in writing outcomes over the 2 years of the project. (The average scaled score growth in NSW public schools in the year of this study was 25.3; the average scaled score growth in this secondary school was 36.4; and other similar schools' average scaled score growth was 15.8).

Finding only one study in Australia that links the explicit teaching of grammar to student learning outcomes suggests a limited focus on these links in Australian research. To incorporate a similar type of intervention in their schools, school leaders can read the Humphrey and Macnaught (2015) study in further detail to find out exactly what type of grammatical knowledge was taught, how the intervention was designed and how it was implemented. More importantly, both the research community and educational and system leaders might consider asking for more research into how the explicit teaching of grammar can raise student writing outcomes.

Strategies to help literacy achievement in your school

The research discussed in the last section provides some evidence for the explicit teaching of grammar within the context of writing in raising student outcomes. No doubt the teaching of grammar separately from the teaching of writing has made no impact on learning outcomes – the findings of meta-analyses since Hillocks (1986) seminal analysis continue to tell us this.

What do Australian curriculum documents suggest? The Australian Curriculum: English (ACARA 2014) states:

> *English uses standard grammatical terminology but applies it within a contextual framework, in which language choices are seen to vary according to the topics at hand, the nature and proximity of the relationships between the language users, and the modes or processes of communication available.* (ACARA 2014)

In other words, the Australian Curriculum tells us that the grammar choices of writers are contextual: specifically based on the topic being discussed, the interpersonal relationships between the language users, and whether the language is written or spoken. This clearly places the explicit teaching of grammar within the writing purpose. As a starting point, school leaders can use the Australian Curriculum and the state-based syllabus documents that align to the view that the explicit teaching of grammar is best taught in the context of language in use.

School leaders may also like to consider the pedagogical direction that has emerged from Myhill, Jones, Watson and Lines (2013). This could provide the link between explicit grammar teaching and language in use and contribute to the raised learning outcomes in both the writing and language elements of NAPLAN. Myhill, Jones, Watson and Lines' (2013) explicit grammar teaching has the potential to expand teachers' pedagogical repertoire around the teaching of grammar and not just their language knowledge, the latter having been the subject of research interventions (Macken-Horarik et al. 2011, 2015; Jones and Chen 2012; Harper and Rennie 2009) in Australia. What did this pedagogical intervention in Myhill and her colleagues' study look like? How can explicit grammar be taught in the context of writing lessons? They call the lessons 'playful' and claim that this pedagogical direction can build learners' confidence to take risks because the stakes are not very high. They suggest that students can 'fool around with language' in a classroom environment where constructive failure is normal (Myhill, Jones, Watson and Lines 2013: 109). The 6 principles outlined in Box 3.1 underpinned the explicit grammar lessons in this intervention.

Box 3.1. The 6 principles that underpin the lesson intervention in Myhill, Jones, Watson and Lines (2013)

1. **Language play, experimentation, risk-taking and games should be actively encouraged.**
   By encouraging experimentation in writing lessons, teachers can help writers to see that language can be assembled in whatever way the writer thinks will be the best choice. The elasticity of language and the possibilities it affords are most important. The notion of playfulness is directly counter to the 'deficit model' of grammar.

2. **Discussion is fundamental in encouraging critical conversations about language and effects.**
   The teacher and the students develop a shared language and a shared talk around what are successful language choices in writing. This can be based on the grammatical terms that are in common use across the school or school system.

3. **Grammatical metalanguage is used, but it is explained through examples.**
   Using grammatical metalanguage to describe the language being used builds both better writing and student metalinguistic knowledge.

4. **The use of 'creative imitation' offers model patterns for students to play with and use in their own writing.**
   Mentor texts are commonly used in primary classrooms where student writers can imitate texts that are recognised as successfully meeting the requirements of the task. A recent publication has provided a book of mentor texts across the curriculum. (Humphrey and Vale 2020)

5. **The use of authentic examples from authentic texts links students to the broader community of writers.**
   A focus on successful grammar use in the mentor text allows writers to explore what successful writers do and the choices they make.

6. **Activities should support students in making choices and being designers of writing.**
   Nurturing students' ability to make informed grammatical choices in their writing helps them to see writing as a process of design.

Another representation of the work of Myhill, Jones, Watson and Lines (2013) is provided in the tiered diagram in Figure 3.2. The figure demonstrates how the student writer's authorial choices when producing written texts rests on mentor texts or texts that contain successful demonstrations of the grammar – grammar that the teacher has previously explicitly taught and that the learners have identified and explicitly talked about. This model brings together recent work (Myhill, Jones, Watson and Lines 2013; Myhill, Jones and Watson 2013) to represent a plan that school leaders can use to design school-based pedagogy.

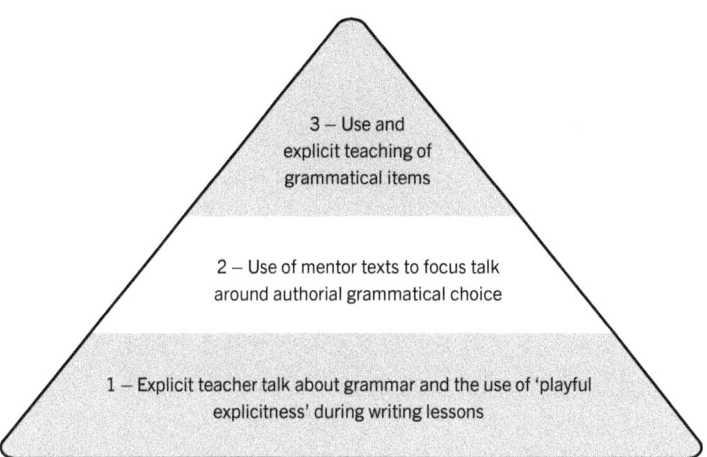

Figure 3.2. Tiered elements of planning for teaching grammar at classroom and school level.

As is made clear in Figure 3.2, knowledge about language 'floats on a sea' of explicit teacher talk about grammar. This is where the teacher has deep and focused knowledge of how and where language works together effectively and can talk about the technical labels and functions of the words in the text. On top of this sit the mentor texts (so called because the texts themselves can teach young writers how to employ the knowledge about language into a final written product), which are thus central features of the teaching of writing. A mentor text can be in the form of a book, a poem, a newspaper article, song lyrics, comic strips, manuals, essays ... almost anything. Dorfman et al. (2017: 7) note that 'mentor texts serve to show, not just tell, students how to write well'.

The 'tip of the triangle' is where the explicit teaching about grammar is supported by the work in the lower parts of the triangle. This is where intense and short learning episodes pay off for school leaders in terms of improving writing scores. This pedagogical leadership might follow this learning sequence: build the talk around texts, be 'playful' with grammar, engage with successful mentor texts, and teach explicit and text-focused grammar. This learning sequence is applicable to young writers just beginning with writing tasks through to more sophisticated writers preparing high-stakes texts for assessment or examination. The final step in the sequence might also be what is known in schools as 'traditional' or 'didactic' teaching sessions, where a particular grammatical item is taught.

Reflections from school leaders

This is from David Partridge, who is an English and history teacher and Head Teacher, Professional Learning at Armidale Secondary College in NSW. He has many years of experience in considering how school leaders can support teachers in raising student outcomes. His reflection points to school leaders building learning communities and communities of practice in their schools to help raise student learning outcomes.

Question 1: What does a school-based approach to an explicit teaching of grammar look like?

Effective school-based approaches to an explicit teaching of grammar are whole school in nature. In the secondary setting, it is not just the work of the subject English teachers, and in the primary setting, it is not isolated to one stage. A school-based approach is collaborative and transformative, informed by cycles of action learning.

Effective school-based approaches are data driven, consisting of much more than assessment outcomes from standardised tests and formal assessment tasks, but rather, the triangulation of data sources, such as student work samples and student wellbeing and engagement data. As educators, we know that when students can access the curriculum, they find learning more meaningful, enjoyable and rewarding.

A focus on an explicit teaching of grammar is responsive to student need and school context and is unrelenting. Effective mining of data informs what aspect of grammar will inform the focus of the program. By developing and presenting a case for change to the school community and ensuring teachers are aware of the moral imperative to commit to improved practice and student learning outcomes, all teachers are committed to the program, increasing teacher agency for taking ownership of the explicit teaching of grammar.

Making time for the planning of an explicit teaching of grammar is essential for a whole-school approach to work. This means working smarter within the school week to find opportunities for professional learning communities/teams to meet, as well as the school executive dedicating resources, both human and financial, to the initiative. Working internally with colleagues using authentic school data sources informs a cycle of meaningful planning, implementation and review.

In professional learning communities, teachers backward map the curriculum, determining the key concepts and skills that are to be developed and how this will be assessed. For an explicit teaching of grammar, this requires the strategic planning of the target text-type and what subject-specific language and language features are to be taught. Complementing this is the explicit teaching of grammar features that underpin this learning and support students to critically deconstruct and construct texts. This process can be enriched through a planned program of lesson observation.

Question 2: Do you think that a whole-school focus on explicit teaching of grammar can contribute to raising student achievement?

Maintaining an explicit focus on grammar in a school's curriculum aids in ensuring there is ongoing professional learning in this space and that this learning translates to improved classroom practice and improved student learning outcomes. It cannot be a program that appears for a year and then goes away. Programs need a gestation period of 4 to 6 years to ensure sustainability and ongoing positive impacts on student learning and teacher practice.

Underpinning students' ability to become accomplished writers is mastery of grammar. It aids students to perform in standardised tests, such as NAPLAN, and also supports students to access the higher bands in HSC examinations, as well as enriching student writing and communication skills more generally. In many HSC courses, for example, English, students are inhibited from accessing the highest band unless they can demonstrate skilful control of language and structure – detailed grammatical knowledge and the ability to implement this in writing is essential to achieve this. Effective explicit teaching of grammar thus aids students to become effective communicators and critical thinkers, enhancing their achievement in these types of standardised assessments.

An explicit focus on grammar is important because it is about communication – knowledge of how to communicate in standard forms empowers students to engage with their world, whether this is their community, politics, media, employment, etc. A whole-school approach on explicitly teaching grammar enables students to interact with the world around them as critical communicators and thinkers. A whole-school focus on the explicit teaching of grammar is therefore a matter of equity, not just achievement.

School-wide improvement

It is useful here to return to Myhill's (2010) work about grammar as a tool for advancing writing and to the wider review of research in the earlier section about whether deficit grammar teaching or grammar teaching 'in context' supports writing achievement. It is the purpose of this chapter and the tiered model presented in Figure 3.2 earlier to suggest that teaching grammar in context with the use of mentor texts is the best way. Taking a sociocultural view of learning to become a meaning maker, as Csikszentmihalyi and Csikszentmihalyi (1992) argue, we can think about the idea that when children are learning to write, they learn more than the system of writing; they learn about the social practices of language. The investment in explicit teacher talk about grammar, both in an explicit and almost playful way, together with the more focused formal teaching of grammar items, can only pay dividends across the whole span of school achievement.

Thus, the question that has emerged is 'which grammar'? Should schools use the grammar that underpins their jurisdictional syllabus? Or the model of language that 'holds sway' in their school or school cluster? Or the model of language that teachers are comfortable with and knowledgeable about? The role for the school leader is to be aware of the grammar used in their school and the level of expertise in grammar across their school. Often though, in practice, schools do not have a shared grammar, or they work from an implicitly agreed understanding of verbs, nouns, prepositions and other descriptive linguistic terms. Many times, this knowledge emerges from teachers' own primary school education. My own research (Cox 2001) demonstrated that almost two-thirds of the upper primary teachers in my study were teaching grammar using the grammatical knowledge that they had learnt in primary classrooms. This teaching was ad hoc and was often without close planning in relation to the writing task that the teachers had assigned to students.

One of the greatest challenges for school leaders is to navigate and lead school programs in grammar, or broader programs around literacy, with a focus on the knowledge about language required for success. One way forward for a school leader would be to use the form and elements of grammar outlined in curriculum documents. The problem with this is that the technical aspects of grammar are difficult to find in a syllabus or curriculum document.

A school leader should ensure that there is an open discussion about grammar just as there would be around other areas of the curriculum. They should also ensure that, where appropriate, a whole-school decision about the form of grammar to be used is linked to guidelines in the relevant syllabus documentation. Supporting this might be classroom textbooks or instructional materials. For teachers like those in my (Cox 2001) study, who are drawing on grammar from their own school learning, the last 20 years has seen a focus on both initial teacher education and professional learning, for teachers to become more familiar with grammar linked to classroom writing tasks. Many research projects, teacher books and professional learning courses have brought individual teachers and groups of teachers in schools to a higher level of expertise than has been known in recent times.

ANNOTATED BIBLIOGRAPHY

Derewianka B and Jones P (2016) *Teaching language in context*, Oxford University Press, New York.

>This book provides a very clear pedagogical model to plan and implement at classroom or school level. It gives metalanguage details to support teachers in talking about texts, including appreciating and creating story worlds, recounting what happened, observing and describing the world, explaining how and why, persuading others, responding, and inquiring.

Humphrey S, Droga L and Feez S (2012) *Grammar and meaning*, Primary English Teaching Association of Australia, Newtown, NSW.

>This book provides teachers with support in planning for explicit talk about metalanguage, focusing on language for expressing ideas, connecting ideas and language for interacting with others.

Humphrey S and Vale E (2020) *Investigating model texts for learning*, Primary English Teaching Association of Australia, Newtown, NSW.

>The book helps us in identifying model texts to work with in classrooms and solves the problem of teachers finding just the right model text to teach writing. The book also provides a series of useful and typical mentor texts for classroom use.

Parkin B and Harper H (2018) *Teaching with intent: scaffolding academic language with marginalised students*, Primary English Teaching Association of Australia, Newtown, NSW.

>With a focus on the power of academic language though the discipline of science, teachers are guided through the process of placing language knowledge at the centre of the writing pedagogy in their classrooms.

Parkin B and Harper H (2019) *Teaching with intent 2: literature-based literacy teaching and learning*, Primary English Teaching Association of Australia, Newtown, NSW.

>This book gives teachers a sequence of pedagogical strategies that allows them to carefully build their students' knowledge about text, language, reading and writing. With many students struggling to decode and draw inferential meaning from text, this book uses storytelling as a highly effective approach to teaching language and literacy.

REFERENCES

ACARA (Australian Curriculum, Assessment and Reporting Authority) (2014) F–10 curriculum, English, Key ideas, ACARA website, accessed 8 March 2022. https://www.australiancurriculum.edu.au/f-10-curriculum/english/key-ideas/

Cox R (2001) *Knowledge about language: system and pedagogy* [unpublished PhD thesis], James Cook University.

Csikszentmihalyi M and Csikszentmihalyi IS (eds) (1992) *Optimal experience: psychological studies of flow in consciousness*, Cambridge University Press, Cambridge.

Derewianka B and Jones P (2016) *Teaching language in context*, Oxford University Press, New York.

Dorfman LR, Cappelli R and Hoyt L (2017) *Mentor texts: teaching writing through children's literature, K–6*, Stenhouse Publishers, Portsmouth, NH.

Fearn L and Farnan N (2005) *An investigation of the influence of teaching grammar in writing to accomplish an influence on writing*, paper presented at the annual meeting of the American Educational Research Association, Montreal, Quebec, Canada.

Graham S, McKeown D, Kiuhara S and Harris KR (2012) 'A meta-analysis of writing instruction for students in the elementary grades', *Journal of Educational Psychology*, 104(4):879–896. http://dx.doi.org/10.1037/a0029185

Graham S and Perin D (2007) 'A meta-analysis of writing instruction for adolescent students', *Journal of Educational Psychology*, 99(3):445–476. https://doi.org/10.1037/0022-0663.99.3.445

Harper H and Rennie J (2009) '"I had to go out and get myself a book on grammar": a study of pre-service teachers' knowledge about language,' *Australian Journal of Language and Literacy*, 32(1):22–37.

Hillocks G (1986) *Research on written composition: new directions for teaching*, National Conference on Research in English, ERIC Clearinghouse on Reading and Communication Skills, Urbana, IL.

Humphrey S (2017) *Academic literacies in the middle years: a framework for enhancing teacher knowledge and student achievement*, Routledge, New York.

Humphrey S and Feez S (2016) 'Direct instruction fit for purpose: applying a metalinguistic toolkit to enhance creative writing in the early secondary years', *Australian Journal of Language and Literacy*, 39(3):207.

Humphrey S and Macnaught L (2015) 'Functional language instruction and the writing growth of English language learners in the middle years', *TESOL Quarterly*, 50(4):792–816.

Humphrey S and Vale E (2020) *Investigating model texts for learning*, Primary English Teaching Association of Australia, Newtown, NSW.

Jones P and Chen H (2012) 'Teachers' knowledge about language: issues of pedagogy and expertise', *Australian Journal of Language and Literacy*, 35(2):147–172.

Jones S, Myhill D and Bailey T (2013) 'Grammar for writing? An investigation of the effects of contextualised grammar teaching on students' writing', *Reading and Writing*, 26(8):1241–1263.

Koster MP, Tribushinina E, De Jong P and Van den Bergh HH (2015) 'Teaching children to write: a meta-analysis of writing intervention research', *Journal of writing research*, 7(2):299–324.

Macken-Horarik M, Love K and Unsworth L (2011) 'Are grammatics "good enough" for school English in the 21st century: four challenges in realising the potential', *Australian Journal of Language and Literacy*, 34(1):9–23.

Macken-Horarik M, Sandiford C, Love K and Unsworth L (2015) 'New ways of working "with grammar in mind" in school English: insights from systemic functional grammatics', *Linguistics and Education*, 31:145–158.

Myhill D (2010) 'Ways of knowing: grammar as a tool for developing writing', in Locke T (ed) *Beyond the grammar wars*, Routledge, New York.

Myhill D and Fisher R (2010) 'Writing development: cognitive, sociocultural, linguistic perspectives', *Journal of Research in Reading*, 33(1):1–3.

Myhill D, Jones S, Lines H and Watson A (2012) 'Re-thinking grammar: the impact of embedded grammar teaching on students' writing and students' metalinguistic understanding', *Research Papers in Education*, 27:2:139–166.

Myhill D, Jones S and Watson A (2013) 'Grammar matters: how teachers' grammatical knowledge impacts on the teaching of writing', *Teaching and Teacher Education*, 36:77–91.

Myhill D, Jones S, Watson A and Lines H (2013) 'Playful explicitness with grammar: a pedagogy for writing', *Literacy*, 47(2):103–111.

Pearson PD and Gallagher MC (1983) 'The instruction of reading comprehension', *Contemporary Educational Psychology*, 8(3):317–344.

CHAPTER 4

Explicit vocabulary instruction

Introduction

Teaching isolated words to those learning to read and write has been seen as unnecessary or even theoretically 'out of fashion'. The 'language experience approach', which was in part derived from the 'growth model' of teaching English (Dixon 1967), recognised that new words are learnt during the process of using and developing English literacy and oracy. For learners whose first language was English and who came from highly literate homes, this was indeed a 'fool-proof' system. Research during the 1970s when the language experience approach was important described learners as developing their own 'linguistic data pool' (Harste and Burke 1977) – a model where each language encounter feeds into a common pool of linguistic data, from which a learner can draw in a subsequent language encounter. This theory suggested that teaching vocabulary was not necessary because everyone would build their own data pool, naturally and through experience. However, research by Anderson and Freebody (1982) demonstrated that students who do not know all-purpose academic words, such as communicate, respond, local, common, global and support, struggle with comprehension of texts containing these words (National Research Council 2003). Anderson and Freebody (1982) proposed that many language experience approach methods do not encompass these all-purpose academic words.

Theories such as Harste and Burke's (1977) 'linguistic data pool' have not considered contexts where English is not historically the first language, or the changing populations of classrooms following increased immigration that has resulted in many students in our schools speaking English as an additional language or dialect. *World Englishes* was described by Crystal (1978) and others as the different varieties of English and English-based creoles that developed in different regions of the world – see Trudgill and Hannah (2008) for a comprehensive overview. Taking account of changes in vocabulary use associated with social changes and the immigration patterns associated with globalisation, today we have moved, as in many other aspects of English language and literacy teaching, into a more explicit form of vocabulary instruction.

How explicit vocabulary instruction can support achievement in literacy

Research around the success of different forms of explicit vocabulary instruction has a long and rich history, which begins with some empirical studies (Carroll 1971; Freebody and Anderson 1983a; Freebody and Anderson 1983b) demonstrating a strong link between vocabulary knowledge and reading comprehension scores. These studies promoted the teaching of vocabulary definitions, dictionary work and the teaching of synonyms and antonyms, often completely without connection to the word in use or specifically linked to the reading comprehension processes. Further research (NICHD 2000; Wright and Cervetti 2017) suggested that the 'cold' teaching and learning of vocabulary was not providing the gains in reading comprehension that were promised earlier. So, while the link between vocabulary teaching and increased reading comprehension scores was strongly established, there was a need to consider a more engaging pedagogy beyond that labelled as 'cold' teaching. This led to work that sought to expand the ways in which vocabulary is taught and to consider more about the function of the words being taught.

Both word knowledge and vocabulary instruction increased in popularity, as a pedagogical direction to support learners' achievement in literacy gained focus over time. Empirical research showed successful results in practical interventions in schools, most notably through studies such as those by Snow et al. (2009) and Lawrence et al. (2015), which claimed that the most important words that students need to be taught are those that are crucial to their comprehension of their assigned texts. These words should not be the technical words required in individual lessons but rather, all-purpose academic words central to understanding texts within a sequence of topics (Snow et al. 2009: 327).

The 'Word Generation' program (Snow et al. 2009) is a focused program over time where the objective is to ensure that students:

> encounter the target word in semantically rich contexts in motivating texts
> have recurrent exposure to the word in varying contexts
> have opportunities to use the word orally and in writing
> receive explicit instruction in word meaning
> receive explicit instruction in word learning strategies, for example, morphological analysis, cognate use, polysemy. (Snow et al. 2009: 327)

Post-test findings of an early study of the implementation of a Word Generation program (Lawrence et al. 2010) showed that students learnt approximately the same number of words that differentiated the scores of 6th and 8th graders on the pre test – in other words, participation in 20 to 22 weeks of the program was equivalent to 2 years of learning during business as usual (Lawrence et al. 2010: 23).

In 2015, along with my colleagues, I conducted a local adaptation of this study in 17 multilingual Sydney primary and secondary schools over a period of 10 weeks, using an amended version of the Word

Generation program (Cox et al. 2015). This program focused on word consciousness across curriculum areas and found that across both cohorts of students in Year 5 and Year 7, there was a gain in vocabulary knowledge between the pre tests and the post tests.

The average raw score results at Year 5 identified a gain in all word knowledge learning between the pre and post tests and, in this cohort, girls outperformed boys. Analysis at school level showed that all the 8 primary schools registered a gain, with some schools showing a gain of as much as 21 per cent following the explicit teaching of vocabulary knowledge in the intervention. In Year 7, there were also gains, but they were not of the same magnitude as those in the primary school. Analysis at school level showed that all but one of the 9 schools made a gain between the pre and post test results. Clearly, there is evidence from these descriptive statistics that the implementation of the Word Generation program in these urban multilingual Australian schools improved vocabulary knowledge.

Another approach to the best way of teaching new vocabulary is evident in the work of Nagy et al. (2002). They looked at the function of the words being taught, and focused on the complexity of word knowledge, demonstrating that procedural knowledge of a word is more important than an ability to have declarative knowledge of a word (Nagy et al. 2002). This suggests that knowing the word is not as important as knowing how to use the word and that knowing a word is more subtle than just being able to give a definition. Many small experimental studies have also given us clear evidence of a series of instructional factors that promote successful vocabulary learning (Beck et al. 2013; Beck et al. 1982; Graves 2006; NICHD 2000; Stahl and Nagy 2006). These instructional factors are summarised in Table 4.1.

Table 4.1. Features of instructional factors that promote vocabulary learning

INSTRUCTIONAL FACTORS	FEATURES
incrementality	knowledge of a word grows gradually, increasingly approximating mature understanding
polysemy	word meanings are inherently flexible, with multiple senses and nuances
multidimensionality	words have multiple forms and features, such as spoken, written, grammatical, collocational behaviour, and associations with other words
interrelatedness	e.g. learning *cool* is easier if you know *hot*, *cold*, and *warm*
heterogeneity	essential knowledge about a specific word depends on the type of word it is

Further aspects of vocabulary instruction have emerged from research (Beck et al. 2013) and one that is commonly used in school programs and classroom practice involves dividing words into 3 tiers. Researchers argue that the most important words to be explicitly taught in primary schools are those from tier 2, for learners to be ready for instruction in tier 3 words in secondary school.

Tier 1 consists of the most basic words – *clock, baby, happy* – and for students whose families speak English at home, these rarely require instruction in school. Explicit instruction in tier 1 words is required for students who enter school from an EAL/D background.

Tier 2 are high frequency words for mature language users – *coincidence, absurd, industrious* – these words can be taught and can add productively to a learner's language ability.

Tier 3 are words with low frequency – *lathe, isotope, peninsula* – and are probably best learnt when needed in a content area. (Beck et al. 2013)

Strategies to help literacy achievement in your school

The opening section of this chapter has focused specifically on the well-researched field of vocabulary instruction. Vocabulary instruction is one of the 5 pillars of reading so strongly advocated in the National Reading Panel's (NICHD 2000) meta-analysis and is commonly regarded a high-impact practice for school leaders. However, this section of the chapter steps a little beyond accepting the need for teaching vocabulary knowledge explicitly and explores what might be the best evidence-based way of teaching vocabulary knowledge.

For school leaders, it is important that early years teachers value the essential place of talk for social interactive reasons in the classroom, and that they understand how the movement from this social function to the integration into explicit teaching of early literacy skills and knowledge can support all learners. This has been covered in detail in Chapter 2, which gives some evidence-based reasons for the importance of oral language as well as some directions for school leaders to lead this at a school level.

Recently, there has been a new wave of vocabulary research that looks more closely at the 'sub-word' level of meaning. In English, we often describe the language by talking about 3 systems. These are:

1. the sound–symbol aspects of language structure (grapho–phonic relationships)

2. the meaning aspects of language structure (morphological relationships)

3. the grammatical aspects of language structure (syntactical relationships).

This way of describing language, particularly in the teaching of early reading (see Chapter 5), is now somewhat contested and could fill another book. However, for the purpose of this discussion, it is useful.

The teaching of reading requires students to understand and exploit each of the 3 systems simultaneously to both read and understand what they are reading. Recent research into teaching and learning vocabulary emphasises the centrality of the second system, or the morphologic system of language. For example, Bowers and Kirby (2010) provide evidence that morphologic vocabulary instruction (instruction using sets of morphologically related words to teach how to find meaning cues in consistent spelling patterns) is an effective way of increasing vocabulary knowledge among primary-aged learners.

The core elements of the program devised by Bowers and Kirby (2010) are:

1. English spelling is a highly consistent system for representing the meaning of words. Few words fail to follow established conventions for this purpose.

2. Morphemes (bases, prefixes and suffixes) are the smallest units in a word that carry meaning. Morphemes can be combined and recombined to form many words like LEGO pieces are rearranged into countless structures.

3. Bases, prefixes, and suffixes maintain consistent spellings in words regardless of shifts in pronunciation. Spelling changes occur across derivations according to consistent suffixing patterns. (Bowers and Kirby 2010: 332)

Bowers and Kirby's (2010) study used a 20-lesson classroom intervention for Grades 4 and 5 students that taught morphological analysis, knowledge and skills, to develop vocabulary beyond the words the students were taught, but not beyond the morphological families (or groups of words that have similar meanings). The results of this study showed that teaching Grades 4 and 5 students how morphology works improved their ability to 'peel' affixes off complex words and allowed them to build their vocabulary knowledge independent of teacher instruction. Bowers and Kirby (2010) point out that teaching morphological analysis skills may make it easier for students to recognise a base they know in large complex words that could otherwise be missed. This is in contrast with other approaches to vocabulary instruction (see Biemiller and Boote 2006) that suggest teaching vast numbers of individual vocabulary items in classrooms.

Much recent evidence-based practice suggests that vocabulary instruction is best done in a context of enjoyment and active engagement (see NICHD 2000). The model of Bowers and Bowers (2018: 409) further promotes a focus on the consistent structure of written morphology using problem-solving activities in which learners act as 'word detectives', firmly stating that, 'English prioritizes the consistent spelling of morphemes over the consistent spellings of phonemes'.

Bowers is not alone in recognising the clear connection between vocabulary instruction and spelling instruction. Bowers's other work (see Anderson et al. 2019) looks at the role of morphological knowledge in teaching early reading and spelling and argues strongly that a focus on both morphology and grapho-phonic relationships at the same time is the best way to approach vocabulary instruction. This work and the accompanying website *Beyond the Word* encourage the systematic teaching of morphological analysis as a way of designing vocabulary lessons. Further to this, it provides students with inquiry-based skills in working with words to continue independent learning over time.

As suggested earlier, findings from recent research into the pedagogy of vocabulary instruction point to the movement away from the learning of vocabulary as 'a lone project' undertaken as a form of 'autonomous literacy' (Street 2006). Vocabulary instruction and vocabulary learning is far more about engagement with words and their structure, and words and their meaning. This is reflected in the title *Caught in the spell of words*, the name of a blog by Lyn Anderson and Ann Whiting, which encourages teachers to consider teaching word meanings and spelling together. In this blog, Anderson and Whiting (2020) use words like 'passion for studying words' and 'word nerdery' to consider vocabulary and word study part of the social practice of literacy.

Figure 4.1 provides the key elements of a vocabulary instructional program that might operate across the school and form the basis for grade level planning – one where spelling and vocabulary instruction might go hand in hand with a reading program or writing topics in a writing program.

Explicit vocabulary instruction

CHOOSE THE RIGHT WORDS ← Beck et al. (2002) suggest teaching both topic words and general academic words. These appear in different forms in many content areas, often with varying meanings (e.g. describe, outline, calculate).

ENSURE REPEATED, RICH EXPOSURE ← McKeown et al. (1985) found that students who had 12 instructional encounters with target words learnt the words better than those who had 4. Probably the most consistent finding around good vocabulary instruction is that students need multiple exposures to a word to learn it well (Lawrence 2009; Nagy et al. 1985).

ENCOURAGE VOCABULARY USE AND EXPERIMENTATION ←
- Writing is a great opportunity for improving and consolidating vocabulary, and much research shows that vocabulary is one of the most important features of writing. Muncie (2002: 228) found that 'It appears that during the process of revising their work, students do indeed use a greater proportion of more sophisticated words than in their normal writing'.

TEACH WORD LEARNING STRATEGIES ←
- All students need additional encounters in different contexts to ensure they develop rich orthographic, phonological and semantic knowledge of the word (Perfetti and Hart 2002). Snow et al. (2009) found that students in schools implementing the Word Generation vocabulary teaching program learnt more of the targeted words than those in comparison schools, even though the latter group performed at a higher level before the investigation.

CONSIDER VOCABULARY INSTRUCTION AND SPELLING INSTRUCTION TOGETHER ←
- Apel et al. (2012) found that morphological awareness uniquely contributed to spelling and word recognition and was significant in its unique contribution to reading comprehension. Vocabulary and spelling instruction following analysis can improve spelling ability and reading comprehension and increase reading vocabulary.

Figure 4.1. Evidence-based teaching model for explicit vocabulary instruction

Utilising explicit planning for vocabulary instruction, including selection of key words and ensuring exposure as many times as possible to these words in different contexts across school years, should result in a school community being able to lift word knowledge and vocabulary use over time. An increase in knowing and using words will be noticed by improvement in writing, spelling and reading scores in external tests, but will also be noticed in the increase in subtle understandings in reading both fiction and nonfiction texts.

Most importantly, if spelling and vocabulary instruction are undertaken together using morphological orthography (see Anderson et al. 2019) where spelling lists contain words linked orthographically (through common spelling) and morphologically (through similar meaning), like 'bicycle', 'cycle', and 'circle', students can tackle the 2 jobs of learning meaning and spelling together. They can begin an exploration of words until they are able to develop self-reliance in exploration and application of word learning strategies.

Reflections from school leaders

The following reflection from Monica Palmer, a principal of a Catholic primary school in Sydney, shows us how a school leader has foregrounded the importance of explicit and consistent teaching of vocabulary knowledge across her school.

Question 1: What does a school-based approach to an explicit vocabulary knowledge program look like?

A school-based approach to building vocabulary revolves around embedding new words into explicit classroom instruction as well as utilising the same words frequently in everyday classroom conversation. One successful and motivational program that I have used that considered this rich approach to vocabulary development was the 'Word Generation' program (Snow 2009) for our middle school students. This vocabulary pedagogy has focus on discipline-specific words (tier 3) but also, importantly, academic 'all-purpose' words (tier 2), such as 'function', 'interpret', 'factor', that may appear across a range of disciplines. The inclusion of 'all-purpose' academic words is crucial because if teachers concentrate instruction only on technical vocabulary terms specific to their disciplines, then the more general words may not be explicitly taught.

At our school, explicit instruction for our vocabulary lessons for tier 2 and tier 3 words occurs through daily 'shared reading' lessons where words are experienced in context and meanings and word forms are elaborated upon using carefully considered mentor texts. The students experience frequent exposure to the words in varied contexts and practise vocabulary through planned oral and written engagements.

Planning with a view of vocab across curriculum and grade

At our school, we engage in collaborative planning linked to a range of curriculum areas. As we are a high EAL/D school, our planning always revolves around a focus on pedagogies that support language development, and therefore vocabulary development is featured in our documentation. Based on pre-assessment writing tasks across KLAs [key learning areas], we consider tier 3 and tier 2 words. In the [following] examples, our tier 2 words support writing our generalisations, explanations and hypotheses for our science units. The tables show practical planning document examples where the focus on the vocabulary to teach is noted and considered by function.

VOCABULARY KNOWLEDGE AND LANGUAGE FOCUS NEEDS – MATTER

Tier 2 words
Focus on communicative vocabulary associated with the text type

Causal connectives:
because, due to

Conditional adjectives:
if

Language of description – adjectives, adverbs, adverbial phrases:
durable, sustainable, functional, structural, aesthetically pleasing

Verbs:
separate, combine

Nominalisation:
evaporation, condensation, insulation

Tier 3 words
Focus for teaching technical vocabulary associated with topic

Conceptual vocabulary:
states of matter, solids, liquids, gases, chemistry, materials, properties, structural, functional, particles

Skill based vocabulary:
prediction, manipulate, manage, conduct, producing, evidence, investigate, analyse

VOCABULARY KNOWLEDGE AND LANGUAGE FOCUS NEEDS – GEOGRAPHY

Tier 2 words
Focus on communicative vocabulary associated with the text type

Causal connectives:
because, due to

Conditional connectives:
if

Temporal connectives:
then, next

Tier 3 words
Focus for teaching technical vocabulary associated with topic

Conceptual vocabulary:
shoreline, landforms, erode, Earth, natural, human activity, process, characteristics, rocks, fossils, interactions, rotation, rotate, axis, relationship, relational, day, night, seasonal, orbit, effect, humus, decomposition, micro-organisms, composition.

Skill based vocabulary:
predict, hypothesis, variables (independent and dependent), evaluate, analyse, identify, question, plan, conduct, communicate, data, patterns, trends, collect, represent, fair test, reasons

Explicit vocabulary instruction

VOCABULARY KNOWLEDGE AND LANGUAGE FOCUS NEEDS – CLIMATE

Tier 2 words
Focus on communicative vocabulary associated with the text type

Language of description – adjectives, adverbs, adverbial phrases:
where, when, how

Language of position:
northerly, southerly

Temporal connectives:
next, later, finally

Causal connectives:
because, due to

Tier 3 words
Focus for teaching technical vocabulary associated with topic

Conceptual vocabulary:
sunrise, sunset, phases of the moon, cumulus, rotation, hemispheres, thermometer, rain gauge, velocity, temperature

Skill based vocabulary:
measure, predict, synthesise

VOCABULARY KNOWLEDGE AND LANGUAGE FOCUS NEEDS – LIVING THINGS

Tier 2 words
Focus on communicative vocabulary associated with the text type

Language of description – adjectives, adverbs, adverbial phrases:
quickly, fresh, fast

Verbs:
disperse, fertilise, grow

Temporal connectives:
next, later, finally

Causal connectives:
so, that, because

Tier 3 words
Focus for teaching technical vocabulary associated with topic

Conceptual vocabulary:
stem, stalk, stamen, leaf, roots, pollen, nectar, chrysalis, butterfly, moth, insect

Skill based vocabulary:
observe, measure, compare, contrast

Question 2: Do you think that a whole-school focus on vocabulary knowledge can contribute to raising student achievement?

Another program we have used is the 'detailed reading program' (Rose 2012). This program of reading and writing has increased students' oral, reading and writing achievement. The detailed reading program has a very clear focus on vocabulary development through a focus on using meaning cues for students to identify key words and phrases in a subject specific text. These tier 2 and tier 3 words are identified, highlighted and then meaning and grammar details about the vocabulary highlighted is shared with the students. The highlighted vocabulary is then used as notes to stimulate complex sentence construction about the inferred meaning of the discipline-specific texts studied with the teacher.

[In a table at the end of this reflection,] I have detailed students' ability to access text meaning based on knowledge of vocabulary before and after utilising detailed reading as a strategy. Students' self-efficacy and improved knowledge of vocabulary has assisted their growth in responses to scientific texts. Following this explicit vocabulary teaching (we often ask student writers to respond to the text by answering a pre-prepared question) the exact linguistic requirement is detailed. For example, when a writer reads a text about heating and cooling a home and is asked the question: What are the things to consider when heating and cooling our homes?

With the request that the writer produces 4 complex sentences, here is the response prior to the detailed reading program (Rose 2012) intervention and afterwards, which demonstrate the efficacy and strength of this explicit focus on language structure and vocabulary, together with evidence of conceptual development.

MICHAEL'S TEXT BEFORE INTERVENTION	MICHAEL'S TEXT AFTER INTERVENTION
If your house is built correctly you can use heating or cooling for your house. If you are renovating or planning to it is important to make your house energy efficient from the start. If you are going to use heating, it does not include hot water usage.	You need a well-designed home for a good heating and cooling system all year around. If you have a well-designed home and you have good heating and cooling then you can reduce greenhouse gas emissions. If you have poorly designed windows, skylights and doors can make your house too hot or too cool. So, you need to have a well-designed house. If you are building a new house or renovating your house can be energy efficient from the start. With a well-designed house you can reduce energy bills and have comfort all year round. You can recover costs with savings all year round.

School-wide improvement

Learning vocabulary should no longer only be deemed as an individual pursuit to be acquired through engagement with fiction and nonfiction reading; it can also be acquired via focused lessons on word study, working from the morphological basis of words. Further to this, bringing orthography and morphology together allows for spelling skills to be enhanced by building morphological knowledge of words – that is, meaning is the base of knowing a word and if the morphology is made evident to the learner, then the ability to build vocabulary knowledge can be driven by the learner. Kirby et al. (2009: 530) tell us that 'increasing precise morphological knowledge would support the development of high-quality lexical representations, not just for words, but for families of structurally and meaningfully related words.'

School leaders should also look at how the Australian Curriculum supports what the research is telling us, in that vocabulary knowledge builds incrementally around understandings of how words are constructed from morphological units, and that the grammatical function of a word also adds to the learning of that word. School leaders need to be familiar with Australian Curriculum: English and other state-based syllabi and the place of vocabulary learning and vocabulary knowledge in their relevant jurisdictions. In a similar way, school leaders can refer to results from internal assessment and external measures, such as NAPLAN, to determine success in school-based vocabulary learning in their own contexts.

Vocabulary is commonly regarded as a high-impact practice for school leaders. For a long time, it was thought that the only vocabulary that needed to be taught were the technical words required to complete reading and writing tasks. But school leaders should also consider the more systematic implementation of vocabulary instruction programs (e.g. Word Generation) at a school-wide level.

Teachers know that vocabulary knowledge underpins reading comprehension across the grade levels and the research confirms this.

ANNOTATED BIBLIOGRAPHY

Beck IL, McKeown MG and Kucan L (2013) *Bringing words to life: robust vocabulary instruction*, Guilford Press, New York.

> Grounded in research and put together by trusted experts who draw on experience in diverse classrooms and schools, the book explains how to select words for instruction, introduce their meanings, and create engaging learning activities.

Graves MF (2016) *The vocabulary book: learning and instruction*, Teachers College Press, New York.

> This book provides a 4-part model for vocabulary instruction, which aligns to the research outlined in this chapter. The book is part of a US series that showcases the leading researchers in language and literacy education in that country.

Marzano RJ and Simms JA (2013) *Vocabulary for the common core*, Marzano Research Lab, Denver, CO, Portland, OR.

> North American in content and adjusted to the learning outcomes of the common core curriculum in the US. Part 1 gives a 6-step process for vocabulary instruction and provides a framework for building a school-wide vocabulary program.

Overturf BJ, Montgomery LH and Smith MH (2013) *Word nerds: teaching all students to learn and love vocabulary*, Stenhouse Publishers, Portsmouth, NH.

> This book is about teaching vocabulary in a way that is culturally relevant and engaging and gives strategies for teaching vocabulary as well as 5-day and 10-day planning frameworks.

REFERENCES

Anderson L and Whiting A (2020) 'About', *Caught in the spell of words*, accessed 16 March 2022. https://caughtinthespellofwords.wordpress.com/about/

Anderson L, Whiting A, Bowers P and Venable G (2019) 'Learning to be literate: an orthographic journey with young students', in Cox R, Feez S and Beveridge L (eds) *The alphabetic principle and beyond ... surveying the landscape*, Primary English Teaching Association (PETAA), Newtown, NSW.

Anderson RC and Freebody P (1982) *Reading comprehension and the assessment and acquisition of word knowledge* (Tech. Rep. No. 249), University of Illinois, Center for the Study of Reading, Urbana.

Apel K, Wilson-Fowler EB, Brimo D and Perrin NA (2012) 'Metalinguistic contributions to reading and spelling in second and third grade students', *Reading and Writing*, 25(6):1283–1305.

Beck IL, McKeown MG and Kucan L (2013) *Bringing words to life: robust vocabulary instruction*, Guilford Press, New York.

Beck IL, Perfetti CA and McKeown MG (1982) 'Effects of long-term vocabulary instruction on lexical access and reading comprehension', *Journal of Educational Psychology*, 74(4):506.

Biemiller A and Boote C (2006) 'An effective method for building meaning vocabulary in primary grades', *Journal of Educational Psychology*, 98(1):44.

Bowers JS and Bowers PN (2018) 'Progress in reading instruction requires a better understanding of the English spelling system', *Current Directions in Psychological Science*, 27(6):407–412.

Bowers P and Kirby N (2010) 'Effects of morphological instruction on vocabulary acquisition', *Reading and Writing,* 23(5):515–537.

Carroll JB (1971) *Implications of aptitude test research and psycholinguistic theory for foreign language teaching*, paper presented at XVIIth International Congress, International Association of Applied Psychology, Liege, Belgium.

Cox R, O'Brien K, Walsh M and West H (2015) 'Working with multilingual learners and vocabulary knowledge for secondary schools: developing word consciousness', *English in Australia*, 50(1):77.

Crystal D (1978) 'The analysis of intonation in young children', in Minifie FD and Lloyd LL (eds) *Communication and cognitive abilities-early behavioral assessment*, University Park Press, Baltimore.

Dixon J (1967) *Growth through English*, National Association for the Teaching of English (NATE), Reading, England.

Freebody P and Anderson RC (1983a) 'Effects of vocabulary difficulty, text cohesion, and schema availability on reading comprehension', *Reading Research Quarterly*, 18(3):277–294.

Freebody P and Anderson RC (1983b) 'Effects on text comprehension of differing proportions and locations of difficult vocabulary', *Journal of Reading Behavior*, 15(3):19–39.

Graves MF (2006) 'Building a comprehensive vocabulary program', *New England Reading Association Journal*, 42(2):1.

Harste JC and Burke CL (1977) 'A new hypothesis for reading teacher research: both the teaching and learning of reading is theoretically based', in Pearson PD (ed) *Reading: theory research and practice*, National Reading Conference, New York.

Kirby JR, Bowers PN and Deacon SH (2009) *Effects of instruction in morphology on reading*, paper presented at the biannual meeting of the European Association for Research in Learning and Instruction, Amsterdam, The Netherlands.

Lawrence JF (2009) 'Summer reading: predicting adolescent word learning from aptitude, time spent reading, and text type', *Reading Psychology*, 30(5):445–465.

Lawrence JF, Crosson AC, Paré-Blagoev EJ and Snow CE (2015) 'Word generation randomized trial: discussion mediates the impact of program treatment on academic word learning', *American Educational Research Journal*, 52(4):750–786.

Lawrence JF, White C and Snow CE (2010) 'The words students need', *Educational Leadership*, 68(2):23–26.

Marzano RJ and Simms JA (2013) *Vocabulary for the common core*, Marzano Research Lab, Denver, CO, Portland, OR.

McKeown MG, Beck IL, Omanson RC and Pople MT (1985) 'Some effects of the nature and frequency of vocabulary instruction on the knowledge and use of words', *Reading Research Quarterly*, 20(5):522–535.

Muncie J (2002) 'Process writing and vocabulary development: comparing lexical frequency profiles across drafts', *System*, 30(2):225–235.

Nagy WE, Herman PA and Anderson RC (1985) 'Learning words from context', *Reading Research Quarterly*, 20(2):233–253.

Nagy W and Scott J (2000) 'Vocabulary processes', in Kamil ML, Mosenthal PB, Pearson PD and Barr R (eds) *Handbook of reading research*, 3, Routledge, New York.

National Research Council (2003) *Strategic Education Research Partnership SERP*, The National Academies Press, Washington, DC.

NICHD (National Institute of Child Health and Human Development) (2000) *Report of the National Reading Panel: teaching children to read: reports of the subgroups*. National Institute of Child Health and Human Development, National Institutes of Health, Washington, DC.

Perfetti CA and Hart L (2002) 'The lexical quality hypothesis', *Precursors of Functional Literacy*, 11:67–86.

Rose D (2012) *PETAA paper 2002: engaging and supporting all our students to read and learn from reading*, Primary English Teaching Association of Australia, Newtown, NSW.

Snow CE, Lawrence JF and White C (2009) 'Generating knowledge of academic language among urban middle school students', *Journal of Research on Educational Effectiveness*, 2(4):325–344.

Stahl SA and Nagy WE (2006) *Teaching word meanings*, Erlbaum, Mahwah, NJ.

Street B (2006) 'Autonomous and ideological models of literacy: approaches from new literacy studies', *Media Anthropology Network*, 17–24.

Trudgill P and Hannah J (2008) *International English: a guide to varieties of standard English*, Routledge.

Wright TS and Cervetti GN (2017) 'A systematic review of the research on vocabulary instruction that impacts text comprehension', *Reading Research Quarterly*, 52(2):203–226.

CHAPTER 5

Teaching early reading

Introduction

Without a doubt, 'the jury is in' regarding the research directions in how to teach reading in schools. These directions come from the National Reading Panel report (NICHD 2000), the meta-analysis of the research conducted by the National Institute of Child Health and Development in the US. The report's phrase 'the big five', which was touched on in the last chapter with regard to vocabulary, has become a commonly used way of talking about how to teach reading.

So, what is so important about the announcement of 'the big five' and why is it commonly agreed that this is the right approach to teaching reading? As was outlined in Chapter 1, a meta-analysis is a quantitative research methodology where the results of multiple quantitative studies are reviewed and statistically collated. The outcomes from these reviews are held to be strong evidence of directions for practice. Of course, getting the terms of inclusion in the meta-analysis right is central to this form of evidence, and there are many who have challenged the findings of the report based on the terms of inclusion. These papers are known collectively as the 'smoke and mirrors' papers (see Ehri and Stahl 2001; Garan 2001; Krashen 2005).

How the explicit teaching of reading can support achievement in literacy

Each element of 'the big five' from the National Reading Panel report along with broad findings connected to reading teaching and improvement are presented in Box 5.1.

Box 5.1. 'The big five': evidence from the National Reading Panel (NICHD 2000)

1. **Phonemic awareness**

   Phonemic awareness refers to the ability to focus on and manipulate phonemes in spoken words.

   'Effects were significant on measures of children's ability to read words and pseudowords as well as their reading comprehension. Effects were significant on standardised tests as well as experimenter-devised tests. These findings show that teaching children to manipulate phonemes in words was highly effective across all the literacy domains and outcomes (NICHD 2000:(2)3).'

2. **Phonics instruction**

   Systematic phonics instruction is a way of teaching reading that stresses the acquisition of letter–sound correspondences and their use to read and spell words.

   'Findings provided solid support for the conclusion that systematic* phonics instruction makes a bigger contribution to children's growth in reading than alternative programs providing unsystematic or no phonics instruction (NICHD 2000:(2)132).'

3. **Fluency**

   Fluency depends upon well-developed word recognition skills and there is common agreement that fluency develops from reading practice. But there is conflict around the best way to teach fluency.

   For example, (i) to have students read passages orally with teacher feedback (e.g. shared reading), OR (ii) to encourage students to read extensively on their own or with minimal guidance and feedback. (e.g. DEAR – drop everything and read).

'An extensive review of the literature indicates that classroom practices that encourage repeated oral reading with feedback and guidance leads to meaningful improvements in reading expertise for students – for good readers as well as those who are experiencing difficulties (NICHD 2000:(3)3).'

4. **Vocabulary knowledge**

   The importance of vocabulary knowledge in learning to read is usually attributed to Davis (1942), who presented evidence that comprehension comprised 2 'skills': word knowledge or vocabulary and reasoning in reading.

   'Vocabulary occupies an important position in learning to read. As a learner begins to read, reading vocabulary encountered in texts is mapped onto the oral vocabulary the learner brings to the task. The reader learns to translate the (relatively) unfamiliar words in print into speech, with the expectation that the speech forms will be easier to comprehend. Benefits in understanding text by applying letter-sound correspondences to printed material come about only if the target word is in the learner's oral vocabulary. When the word is not in the learner's oral vocabulary, it will not be understood when it occurs in print (NICHD 2000:(3)4).'

5. **Reading comprehension**

   Reading comprehension is a cognitive process that integrates complex skills and 'active interactive strategic processes', which are critically necessary to the development of reading comprehension.

   'Multiple strategy instruction that is flexible as to which strategies are used and when they are taught over the course of a reading session provides a natural basis for teachers and readers to interact over texts (NICHD 2000:(4)46).'

   'These comprehension strategies yield increases in measures of near transfer such as recall, question answering and generation, and summarization of texts (NICHD 2000:(4)51).'

   'The Panel regards this development as the most important finding of the Panel's review because it moves from the laboratory to the classroom and prepares teachers to teach strategies in ways that are effective and natural (NICHD 2000:(4)52).'

*The use of the term systematic phonics does not point to any program but rather underscores that systematic phonics approaches use a planned, sequential introduction of a set of phonic elements along with teaching and practice of those elements.

Recently, in Australia, the work of Konza (2011, 2014), Konza and Main (2015) and Konza and Woodley (2013) have added a sixth dimension to the big five. Konza (2011, 2014) argues very strongly (as does this book in Chapter 2) that the contribution of early oral language development to longer term literacy outcomes for students is important. Teachers also need to support and make the most of all learners' opportunities to develop independent reading skills on the basis of oral language skills (Konza 2011). Even the NRP (NICHD 2000) report itself draws attention to the role of the learner's oral language skills, in particular, oral vocabulary knowledge.

Syllabus documents and The Australian Curriculum foreground oral language in early schooling stages to ensure that oral language development goes hand in hand with literacy development from the early stages to later in school. Australian education systems have, since the 1960s, had a strong focus on oral language. This originated in the 'oracy' movement in the United Kingdom through the work of Wilkinson (1970) and Britton (1970) and is also evident in the recent dialogic classroom work of Alexander (2008) and Mercer et al. (2019). Figure 5.1 represents these ideas graphically.

Teaching early reading

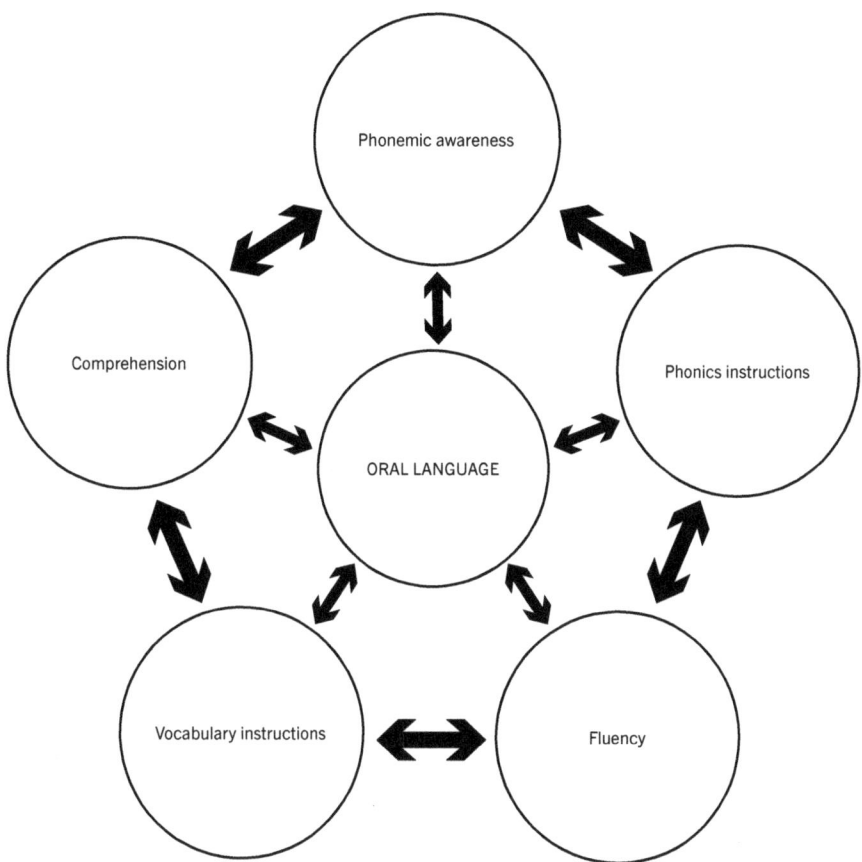

Figure 5.1. Oral language and 'the big five' reading elements (NICHD 2000; Konza 2014)

Since 2000, some of the outcomes of the NRP's influential report have also been supported and elaborated by other reports throughout the English-speaking world. These include:

> *Teaching reading: literature review: a review of the evidence-based research literature on approaches to the teaching of literacy* (Rowe K and NITL [Australia] 2005)

> *British independent review of the teaching of early reading* (Rose 2006)

> *Developing early literacy: a scientific synthesis of early literacy development and implications for intervention* (NELP 2008).

101

Each of these reports provides further leadership to schools and systems in how to organise and plan for the teaching of reading in schools. There is no doubt that teachers, school leaders and school systems have recognised this way of having professional conversations about reading programs and about ensuring that evidence-based practice in the teaching of early reading is foregrounded in schools.

While practice communities have embraced the big five, other theorists and researchers have paused and considered the more far-reaching implications of this blueprint for teaching early reading. Paris (2005) suggests that an area of concern is that all skills are regarded as similar in scope, importance and ability and that the notion of 5 essential skills does not attend to the individual differences of each skill. Classroom teachers and school leaders would know that the idea that each of the 5 elements are equally important and that they are learnt and taught in a similar fashion is just not so. They would also be aware that it is the early years that focus much more on the first 2 of the big five – phonemic awareness and phonics instruction. The remaining 3 skills are built on in the later years of school and, some would argue, are continually learnt and fine-tuned as literacy skills develop over the lifetime.

Paris's (2005: 187) main arguments are clarified when he says, 'There has been relatively less research and classroom emphasis on vocabulary and comprehension to date, perhaps because of the difficulty assessing and teaching these skills to children who are beginning to read.' He suggests that children need to master grapho–phonic relationships (symbol and sound relationships) before being able to read, albeit that some are learnt earlier than others, and that eventually, alphabetic knowledge is mastered but the skills of comprehension are learnt over time (Paris 2005). Further to this, he argues that some skills learnt are dependent on or learnt concurrently with others. Paris (2005) employs the labels: unequal learning, mastery, universality and co-dependency, suggesting that some skills are constrained – learnt and mastered at the early stages of learning to read, whereas others are continually learnt during school and beyond. Taking Paris's (2005) construct a little further, we could conceptualise the big five as being broadly constrained or unconstrained skills. This is depicted in Figure 5.2.

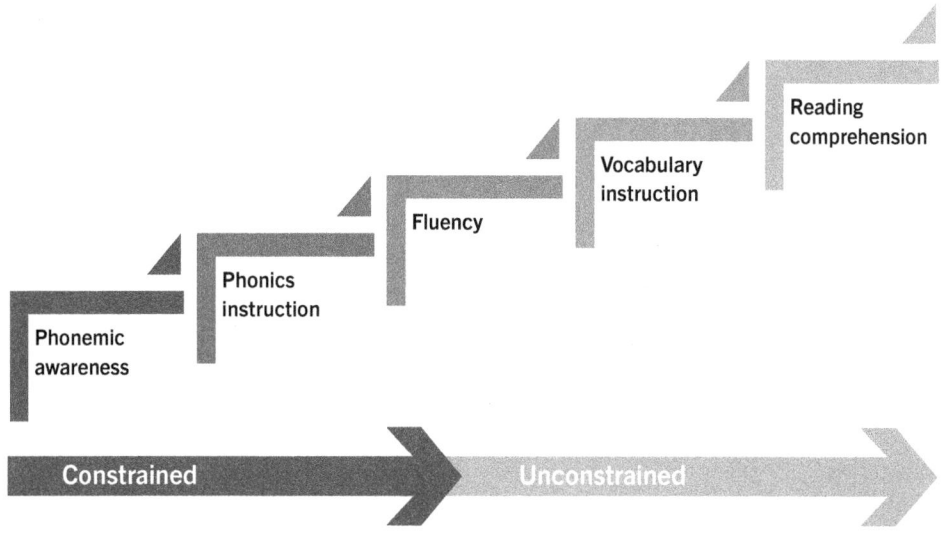

Figure 5.2. The big five (NICHD 2000) as constrained or unconstrained skills

Given that we have a strong evidential base for the teaching of reading and a sense that some of the big five skills are mastered early and others over a longer period of time, it might be useful to consider what the research evidence says. Research by Huck (1977) found that there are 5 main ways that children's books are utilised in reading programs in US schools:

1. the read aloud program
2. the provision for wide reading
3. in-depth discussion groups
4. the use of literature across the curriculum
5. the provision for varied response to books.

These early pedagogical directions identified by Huck (1977) have remained steadfastly in classroom practice in various forms (see Raphael and McMahon 1994; Elley et al. 1996; Rushton et al. 2018).

Many teachers will also be familiar with Pearson and Gallagher's (1983) 'gradual release of responsibility model', sometimes known in schools as '*I do, we do, you do*', which is a source of the focus on pedagogical models for reading lessons. This model is derived from research into the best instructional models for teaching reading comprehension. Lessons will often have the following 4 components: (i) modelled reading, (ii) shared reading, (iii) guided reading and (iv) independent reading.

We have seen a continued connection to the use of 'real books' in classroom reading programs and the emergence of levelled reading programs. Levelled readers are commercially produced reading schemes, where early readers progress through a large scheme of reading books that are levelled for vocabulary complexity, sentence complexity and content interest, for example, PM, Fast Forward, and Oxford Reading Tree readers. In levelled reading programs, teachers pair children with books that best match their reading abilities and as these children's reading skills improve, teachers assign them more complex books. A significant outcome of the almost universal use of commercial levelled reading programs was when publishers noted what teachers were using in their reading classrooms and began to develop levelled readers that reflected the 'real world of books'. Evidence suggests that these reading programs are used comprehensively in schools in Australia and have been for 30 to 40 years. International research that has considered reading pedagogy over time goes as far to suggest:

> *In some schools basals (reading program books) did disappear from classrooms in the late 1980s ... Now, I would say that we have gone full circle, with vocabulary control, especially with the decodability of words presented, dominating commercial reading materials and skills mastery emphasized once again.* (Allington and McGill-Franzen 2000: 142).

Recently in Australia, 'decodable readers' have emerged that provide the strong skills mastery focus on reading materials commonly required by early readers. These decodable readers help children practice a particular letter–sound relationship and reinforce the grapheme and phoneme relationships. There is no doubt that they are very useful in reinforcing sound–symbol relationships. Still, schools need to continue to enrich their reading programs, sustain the overall acquisition of reading skills and maintain a love of reading, through providing the types of reading materials that Huck (1977) spoke about.

Providing a levelled reading program that is evidence based and attracts attention from those interested in theoretically sound reading pedagogy is important. One of the most widely evidenced-based approaches to school and classroom-based reading programs has emerged from the research of Fountas and Pinnell (2001, 2012, 2018). School leaders can take advantage of the deep and engaged development of this approach to school-based literacy – reading and writing taught together over the primary years – now sold to schools as the 'Fountas and Pinnell Literacy Program'. Table 5.1 outlines core elements of the Fountas and Pinnell (2012) reading program.

Table 5.1. Fountas and Pinnell (2012) reading program: core elements

STRATEGY	CLASS TYPE	MATERIALS
guided reading	small group	levelled books
literature discussion	small group, book clubs or whole class	not levelled books
interactive read-aloud	whole class	not levelled books
independent reading with conferences	individual	not levelled books, self-selected
reading minilessons	whole class	not levelled books

Fountas and Pinnell's (2012) program is grounded on levelled readers, yet they strongly argue against the overuse of levelled readers and have never recommended that the school library or classroom libraries be levelled or that levels be reported to parents. They go on to note that level of reading programs should be teachers' tools and should never be a child's label. They tell us, *'Levels are for books, not children'* (Fountas and Pinnell 2012: 281).

There is evidence that 45 per cent of teachers in the US use Fountas and Pinnell's reading program. This is well above the next most popular levelled reading program, which attracts only 27 per cent of teachers (Shwartz 2019), indicating that this comprehensive reading program attracts significant school leader and teacher attention.

Strategies to help literacy achievement in your school

The previous section of this chapter has navigated the broad and deep evidence base for the teaching of reading and there are many other sources where school leaders can read in more depth (see, for example, Wyse and Goswami 2013). This field is large and as the teaching of reading, being such a foundational educational skill, has attracted researcher and practitioner attention over almost 100 years, pulling this evidence base together has not been an easy task. This has been a single 'slice through' the terrain and I apologise if there are some aspects I have under discussed or over emphasised.

This section will show how a strong philosophy and evidence base will afford school leaders a foundation to work from when leading reading programs in schools. This means:

> having a school-based shared philosophy about reading

> being aware of suitable teaching strategies to incorporate across all the school years

> knowing and providing a rich and deep set of reading resources

> providing teaching professional learning support throughout the teaching year

> ensuring that assessment of learners is tied closely to the program that is being implemented and to the philosophy of the school reading program.

If your school-based reading program is designed to reflect the diversity and individuality of your school community, leaving the assessment of reading solely to external instruments or system-wide assessment processes may not provide the optimal data. That is, if your school philosophy is to develop an engaged reading community, standardised tests often assess very basic levels of reading comprehension or vocabulary meanings (as discussed in Chapter 4) and thus only demonstrate the literacy achievement your program is delivering in isolated dimensions. We need to combine this type of evidence with views from a broader lens of reading in the school. There are many systematic ways to do this.

The Australian Curriculum: English (2014) provides an ordered logic of how reading comprehension skills should be taught and anticipated across the primary school years through to early secondary. These are presented in Table 5.2 for school leaders to consider how schools might plan to teach and present these skills in a cumulative manner from early years to lower secondary.

Table 5.2. Reading comprehension skills: early years to lower secondary (ACARA 2014)

EARLY YEARS	MIDDLE PRIMARY	UPPER PRIMARY	LOWER SECONDARY
listens	distinguishes fact from fiction	summarises	–
questions	compares and contrasts	interprets point of view	–
retells	interprets	evaluates point of view	Analyse, explain, evaluate and interpret the ways text structures shape meaning.
recounts	answers inferential questions	evaluates evidence	Interpret, analyse, evaluate and synthesise the information in texts.
infers	evaluates accuracy	generalises	Synthesise ideas in texts.
makes connections	summarises	analyses	Compare, explain and explore text structures and language features in texts.
identifies main idea	interprets main idea		Use and apply prior knowledge. Read increasingly complex texts.

Teachers should use strategies such as shared reading, reading aloud, story discussion circles, one-to-one reading and guided reading groups to teach and reinforce these comprehension skills. Learners in the early years of school can be taught these strategies prior to having complete mastery of the grapho-phonic system or being able to read independently.

The importance of these reading comprehension skills for students through the primary and early secondary years aligns closely to the type of classroom activities. Teachers can and should embed the teaching of these reading comprehension skills into other areas of the curriculum. For example, if we want to teach reading to evaluate accuracy, why not embed that in a science lesson or social science lesson? More examples of this can be found in research such as that of Uccelli and Phillips Galloway (2017) and Swanson et al. (2017).

For a long period, there have been well known instructional sequences for teaching reading comprehension in upper primary school, together with an evidence base of what works best. A good summary of research related to the best strategies for reading comprehension is that presented by Duke and Pearson (2009) who look at the teaching of reading comprehension, which is one of the big five. Duke and Pearson (2009) review the broad range of reading comprehension and teaching strategies that research suggests are effective in classrooms. Figure 5.3 provides an overview of the most common and widely used reading comprehension strategies in schools. It is recommended that these are explained and modelled for students and then emphasised in shared, guided and independent reading.

Prediction
- Students are encouraged to predict what is to come next in the story, how the plot will resolve, or how the factual information might be presented.

Teacher think-aloud
- Teachers use 'think alouds' to demonstrate to students how they as readers engage with the text. A teacher might ask, 'Which animal do I think is going to sink the boat? Will it be the smallest animal or the largest animal?'

Student think-aloud
- Students are asked to think aloud together or individually to ask questions of the text as they read. They can eventually ask these questions 'inside their heads' as they begin to become familiar with engaging in the developing meaning of the text.

Text structure
- Teachers can guide students in mapping how the story complication and resolution are achieved by the author. This works well for narrative texts and picture books.

Visual representations
- Teachers explicitly teach the text structure of factual texts or expository texts. This can be done visually, for example, using graphic organisers, brainstorm charts or semantic maps.

Questions/questioning
- Teachers use questionning to model how compentent readers gain and check meaning from text. Examples are: QAR (question answer relationships), QA (questionning the author), high-level questions of the text (not yes/no answers), look behind the text (questions after reading to understand the author's perspective).

Summarisation
- Teachers need to demonstrate how to read through the text and decide what is important and what is less important and how to make a different version of the text that 'stands for' the original. Teachers might need to carefully consider the purpose of asking learners to summarise a complex narrative. Many deem this as a difficult strategy for children.

Figure 5.3. Instructional strategies for teaching comprehension (Duke and Pearson 2009)

There is a growing body of research and practice suggesting that more explicit scaffolding might best serve readers who come from backgrounds where English may not be the first language or dialect. Sometimes these learners are described as marginalised learners (those who may be from geographically isolated communities, indigenous communities or low socioeconomic communities or have a learning disability). The work comes from a Vygostkian perspective and references Bernstein's (2003) work on the sociology of language and pedagogy. This has most recently been translated into a pedagogical model in Australia by Parkin and Harper (2018, 2019). Educators interested in looking further into the evidence might also consult Gray (2007) Axford et al. (2009), and Derewianka and Jones (2016).

These models suggest that the teacher takes a far more dynamic role and makes explicit the learning goals and how the language and reading skills might be orchestrated by the learner to get the reading task completed. And most importantly, the teacher leads the learning to engage with the text through the text orientation. This text orientation is not a summary of the text, but it orientates the reader to the text. This might be by building content knowledge – for example, if the reader is set in a past time then the text orientation would make this clear; if the characters are from a series of novels then something about the character's life so far might be included; or, if the author is well known for a particular writing style (a good example is Roald Dahl and his invented vocabulary), then this would be a focus in the text orientation. To do this successfully, the onus is on the teacher to actively select a novel where they know the text and the author well. School leaders should also ensure that the library and resources are available.

Following the text orientation, it is suggested that an aural orientation takes place. This is led by the teacher and aims to familiarise learners with the cadence of the language and the sound of fluent reading of a text. These 2 stages reduce 'learner cognitive overload' through the time spent by the teacher in orientating the reader to the meaning and the language before the reading task. Language orientation provides a more focused examination of the language choices that the author has made and why these choices have been made. This has obvious links to the building of skills as writers. The Axford et al.

(2009) model and other similar models place the teacher in an active, dynamic teaching situation that ensures readers are actively engaged in reading and exploring the text for its language, meaning and world view. This is illustrated in Figure 5.4.

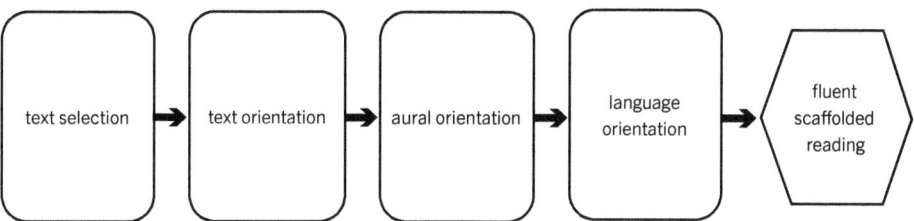

Figure 5.4. Teaching model for reading (based on Axford et al. 2009)

Reflections from school leaders

This is written by Sandra Armstrong, who has been a school leader in various schools in the NSW Department of Education in the Rural North region.

Question 1: What does a school-based approach to an explicit teaching of reading look like?

School leadership is a complex space. Principals lead and manage the school, making organisational and curriculum decisions without being expert in all curriculum areas. The good news is principals do not need to be the expert. They need to be the enabler.

Conducting a situational analysis as part of the school planning cycle offers leaders and their teams the opportunity to assess student need and teacher proficiency. The process shows 'where the school is at' in the teaching of reading and enables students, staff and the school community to be informed and invested. The data gathered is analysed and used to plan an effective school-based approach to the teaching of reading.

Through this process across a number of schools, I have been able to identify those teachers who are expert in the teaching of reading and enable them to become instructional leaders. The instructional leader works at the shoulder with teachers, building their professional capacity through coaching and mentoring. They provide specific feedback on teaching practice and together with the teacher, analyse student reading data and plan student interventions, scaffolds and challenges. The 2 work collaboratively to ensure the teaching of reading is explicit and that assessment of progress occurs regularly. Data gained is used to inform the 'next steps' for teaching and learning.

Question 2: Do you think that a whole-school focus on explicit teaching of reading can contribute to raising student achievement?

Yes. I have seen student outcomes improve as a result of the explicit teaching of reading. A whole-school focus in any curriculum area is the exemplar in achieving optimal student outcomes. Pockets of excellence within a school are not indicative of a whole-school focus.

When you have everyone 'on the bus' and every passenger knowing where they're going and why they're going there, you achieve a whole-school focus. The principal, as the driver, must ensure the road map is clear and that everyone understands the route to be taken. There needs to be regular stops along the way to reflect and take in the view and a celebration for all at the journey's end.

The leadership challenge will always be to ensure that a whole-school focus in one area does not come at the expense of progress in another. Careful and considered forward school planning may assist to buffer against this.

School-wide improvement

Louisa Moats (2020: 3) once said, 'Teaching reading is rocket science'. Our profession needs to recognise how hard it is to develop successful readers and reward ourselves at a job well done. Let us look for a moment at the NAPLAN reading scores from 2009 to 2019. It is difficult to get a statement that clearly outlines the growth or change from 2009 to 2019 at Years 3, 5, 7 and 9. I have developed a graph (Figure 5.5) of the median Australian score for each year level. NAPLAN reading scores range from 1 to 1000 over the 7 years of schooling. Figure 5.5 shows that the scores are stable and high and that in the early years, we have a wider gap between 2009 and 2019. Growth does slow in the secondary years. However, the graph shows that we are teaching reading effectively in schools and we have got better at it in the last 10 years.

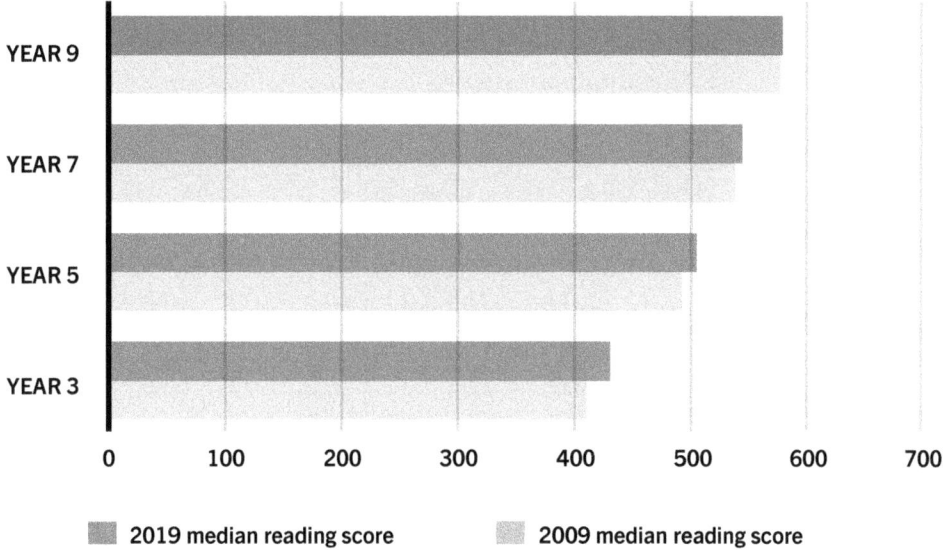

Figure 5.5. NAPLAN reading scores over a 10-year period

Source: 2009 NAPLAN national report and 2019 NAPLAN national report (https://www.nap.edu.au/results-and-reports/national-reports)

Fountas and Pinnell in *Every child, every classroom, every day: from vision to action in literacy learning* (2018) describe 4 key elements of reading. These are elaborated here.

> Element 1: A shared vision and set of core values
>
> School leaders and their teams should make sure that they share a vision for the reading program in the school. It is

useful to address the questions, 'What type of readers do you want in your school?' and, more importantly, 'How does this vision support the requirements for NAPLAN and parental expectations about NAPLAN results?'

› Element 2: Common goals, common language and collective responsibility

When describing the readers in your school, do you have a shared language across teachers, school leaders and even the students themselves? Sharing and recognising expertise in staff, including support staff, is essential to this collective responsibility for success in the school reading program.

› Element 3: A high level of teacher expertise

Often, an experienced teacher with close knowledge of 'this rocket science of teaching reading' is in your team. Recognise and support them. Specifically, the reading recovery teachers may have a high level of expert knowledge that can easily be shared among their colleagues. These teachers can also help you lead the school.

› Element 4: A culture of continuous professional learning

As a school leader, it is important when leading school reading programs and supporting the learning and professional development of your staff that you avoid bandwagons and easy fixes. A long-term professional learning plan for your school allows you to create and sustain shared understanding and goals.

When schools have a shared vision like this, the conversation is lively and expertise and learning among staff are recognised and you will achieve success in your reading program, in your context and in your classrooms.

ANNOTATED BIBLIOGRAPHY

Beck IL, McKeown MG and Kucan L (2013) *Bringing words to life: robust vocabulary instruction*, Guilford Press, New York.

> Grounded in research and put together by trusted experts who draw on experience in diverse classrooms and schools, the book explains how to select words for instruction, introduce their meanings, and create engaging learning activities.

Blevins W (1999) *Phonemic awareness: songs and rhymes*, Scholastic Professional Books, New York.

> Contains activities that are easy to teach and engaging, where children play with sounds through songs, rhymes, poetry, picture games and other exercises. The activities cover the 5 basic levels of phonemic awareness: the ability to hear rhymes and alliteration, to do oddity tasks, to orally blend word and split syllables, to orally segment words, and to do phonemic manipulation tasks.

Cameron S (2009) *Teaching reading comprehension strategies*, Pearson, North Shore.

> Based on compelling evidence that shows that we can improve students' comprehension by the explicit teaching of reading comprehension strategies. This book provides some of the strategies and describes how you go about teaching them in the classroom.

Cox R, Feez S and Beveridge L (2019) *The alphabetic principle and beyond: surveying the landscape*, Primary English Teaching Association (PETAA), Newtown, NSW.

> This book aims to traverse the broad perspectives in the profession about teaching the alphabetic principle. It provides support and confidence for teachers in undertaking this important aspect of teaching early reading. The final chapter is a conversation about a Year 1 lesson from the various perspectives presented in the book.

Elborn S (2015) *Handbook of teaching early reading: more than phonics*, United Kingdom Literacy Association, Leicester.

> An informative research-based book that takes teachers from the early aspects of teaching reading through pedagogical directions and adds comprehension strategies.

Hornsby D and Wilson L (2010) *Teaching phonics in context*, National Council of Teachers of English, Champaign, IL.

> This practical and accessible book demonstrates how explicit systematic teaching of phonics can take place in context, where learning is linked to reading real books.

Pressley M and Allington RL (2014) *Reading instruction that works: the case for balanced teaching*, Guilford Press, New York.

> This well-known teacher resource book demonstrates how successful literacy teachers combine explicit skills instruction with an emphasis on reading for meaning. It is written by 2 of the leading researchers in the field.

REFERENCES

ACARA (Australian Curriculum, Assessment and Reporting Authority) (2014) *Australian Curriculum: English,* ACARA website, accessed 16 March 2022. https://www.australiancurriculum.edu.au/f-10-curriculum/english/

Alexander R (2008) 'Culture, dialogue and learning: notes on an emerging pedagogy', *Exploring Talk in School*, 2008:91–114.

Allington RL and McGill-Franzen A (2000) 'Looking back, looking forward: a conversation about teaching reading in the 21st century', *Reading Research Quarterly*, 35(1):136–153.

Axford B, Harders P and Wise F (2009) *Scaffolding literacy: an integrated and sequential approach to teaching reading, spelling and writing*, ACER Press, Camberwell, VIC.

Beck IL, McKeown MG and Kucan L (2013) *Bringing words to life: robust vocabulary instruction*, Guilford Press, New York.

Bernstein B (2003) *Class, codes and control: applied studies towards a sociology of language*, Volume 2, Psychology Press, East Sussex.

Blevins W (1999) *Phonemic awareness: songs and rhymes*, Scholastic Professional Books, New York.

Britton J (1970) *Language and learning*, Penguin Books, New York.

Cameron S (2009) *Teaching reading comprehension strategies*, Pearson, North Shore.

Cox R, Feez S and Beveridge L (2019) *The alphabetic principle and beyond: surveying the landscape*, Primary English Teaching Association (PETAA), Newtown, NSW.

Davis FB (1942) 'Two new measures of reading ability', *Journal of Educational Psychology*, 33(5):365.

Derewianka B and Jones P (2016) *Teaching language in context*, Oxford University Press, New York.

Duke NK and Pearson PD (2009) 'Effective practices for developing reading comprehension', *Journal of Education*, 189(1/2):107–122.

Ehri L and Stahl SA (2001) 'Beyond the smoke and mirrors: putting out the fire', *Phi Delta Kappan*, 83(1):17–20.

Elborn S (2015) *Handbook of teaching early reading: more than phonics*, United Kingdom Literacy Association, Leicester.

Elley W, Cutting B, Mangubhai F and Hugo C (1996) *Lifting literacy levels with story books: evidence from the South Pacific, Singapore, Sri Lanka, and South Africa*, paper presented at the World Conference on Literacy, Philadelphia, March 12–15.

Fountas IC and Pinnell GS (2001) *Guiding readers and writers, Grades 3-6: teaching comprehension, genre, and content literacy*, Heinemann, Portsmouth, NH.

Fountas IC and Pinnell GS (2012) 'Guided reading: the romance and the reality', *The Reading Teacher*, 66(4):268–284.

Fountas IC and Pinnell GS (2018) 'Every child, every classroom, every day: from vision to action in literacy learning', *The Reading Teacher*, 72(1):7–19.

Garan EM (2001) 'Beyond the smoke and mirrors: a critique of the National Reading Panel report on phonics', *Phi Delta Kappan*, 82(7):500–506.

Gray B (2007) *Accelerating the literacy development of indigenous students: the National Accelerated Literacy Program (NALP)*, Charles Darwin University Press, Melbourne, VIC.

Hornsby D and Wilson L (2010) *Teaching phonics in context*, National Council of Teachers of English, Champaign, IL.

Huck CS (1977) 'Literature as the content of reading', *Theory into practice*, 16(5):363–371.

Konza D (2011) 'Phonological awareness', *Research into practice*, 1(1):1–8.

Konza D (2014) 'Teaching reading: why the "fab five" should be the "big six"', *Australian Journal of Teacher Education (Online)*, 39(12):153.

Konza D and Main S (2015) 'The power of pedagogy: when all else fails', *International Journal of Learning*, Annual Review, 21.

Konza D and Woodley (2013) *Building the systematic teaching of reading across independent schools: 2011–2012: final report*, Fogarty Learning Centre, Edith Cowan University, Joondalup, Australia.

Krashen S (2005) 'Is in-school free reading good for children? Why the National Reading Panel report is (still) wrong', *Phi Delta Kappan*, 86(6):444–447.

Mercer N, Wegerif R and Major L (eds) (2019) *The Routledge international handbook of research on dialogic education*, Routledge, London.

Moats LC (2020) 'Teaching reading is rocket science: what expert teachers of reading should know and be able to do', *American Educator*, 44(2):4.

NELP (National Early Literacy Panel) (2008) *Developing early literacy: a scientific synthesis of early literacy development and implications for intervention*, National Institute for Literacy, Jessup, MA, accessed 16 March. https://lincs.ed.gov/

NICHD (National Institute of Child Health and Human Development) (2000) *Report of the National Reading Panel: teaching children to read: reports of the subgroups*. National Institute of Child Health and Human Development, National Institutes of Health, Washington, DC.

Paris, S. (2005). Reinterpreting the development of reading skills. *Reading Research Quarterly*, 40(2), 184-202.

Parkin B and Harper H (2018) *Teaching with intent: scaffolding academic language with marginalised students*, Primary English Teaching Association (PETAA), Newtown, NSW.

Parkin B and Harper H (2019) *Teaching with intent 2: literature based literacy teaching and learning*, Primary English Teaching Association (PETAA), Newtown, NSW.

Pearson PD and Gallagher MC (1983) 'The instruction of reading comprehension', *Contemporary Educational Psychology*, 8:317–341.

Pressley M and Allington RL (2014) *Reading instruction that works: the case for balanced teaching*, Guilford Press, New York.

Raphael TE and McMahon SI (1994) 'Book club: an alternative framework for reading instruction,' *The Reading Teacher*, 48(2):102–116.

Rose J (2006) *Independent review of the teaching of early reading: final report*, Digital Education Resource Archive (DERA) website, accessed 16 March 2022. https://dera.ioe.ac.uk/5551/

Rowe K and NITL (National Inquiry into the Teaching of Literacy) (Australia) (2005) *Teaching reading – a review of the evidence-based research literature on approaches to the teaching of literacy, particularly those that are effective in assisting students with reading difficulties*, Department of Education, Science and Training, Canberra, Australia.

Rushton K, Ewing R and Diamond M (2018) 'Why real stories matter in learning to read', *Professional Educator*, (Special edition), 14.

Swanson E, Wanzek J, Vaughn S, Fall AM, Roberts G, Hall C and Miller VL (2017) 'Middle school reading comprehension and content learning intervention for below-average readers', *Reading & Writing Quarterly*, 33(1):37–53.

Uccelli P and Phillips Galloway E (2017) 'Academic language across content areas: lessons from an innovative assessment and from students' reflections about language', *Journal of Adolescent & Adult Literacy*, 60(4):395–404.

Wilkinson A (1970) 'The concept of oracy', *The English Journal*, 59(1):71–77.

Wyse D and Goswami U (2013) 'Early reading development', *The SAGE handbook of early childhood literacy*, 523-540.

CHAPTER 6

Intervention and supporting literacy learners

Introduction

While the previous chapters have explored the key elements of literacy and ways in which to best teach these to assist students to achieve their full potential, there will always be students who need extra support in this essential area of learning. School leaders play a critical role in implementing best practice methods for leading literacy improvement across the school cohort, particularly for students who require further assistance.

Diagnostic assessment and tailored intervention can provide a platform for a school leader to lead instructional change and bring about a rise in literacy achievement. In recent years, research in the leadership area has provided a basis for considering the role of school leaders as central to instructional change.

As most school leaders must lead across the full curriculum and lead the organisation and structure of the school for staff, students and families, the task is a substantial one. This chapter proposes that the school leader works in a literacy teaching community of practice (Lave and Wenger 1991). There, they enact what Ogawa and Bossert (1995) describe as leadership that is not confined to certain roles in organisations, but which flows through the networks of roles that comprise organisations. Previous chapters have reminded school leaders that teachers are often familiar with (and at times, expert in) high-impact practices that they know raise achievement in the learners in their classes. Childs-Bowen et al. (2000: 28) hold the view that

> *teachers are leaders when they function in professional learning communities to affect student learning; contribute to school improvement; inspire excellence in practice; and empower stakeholders to participate in educational improvement.*

How diagnostic assessment and tailored intervention can support achievement in literacy

ASSESSMENT

So, what does research say about the place of diagnostic assessment in literacy? Alderson (2005) suggests that diagnostic tests should identify strengths and weaknesses in learners' use of language and should focus on specific elements rather than global abilities. Scholars like Alderson (2005: 2) ask us as a language and literacy teaching community to 'start a debate about how diagnostic testing might most appropriately be developed', arguing that 'the field has neglected to construct diagnostic tests, partly because other forms of testing – in particular high-stakes testing – have dominated the field'.

Assessment of learning outcomes is driven by its purpose. Since the 1990s, consecutive governments in Australia, in a search to ensure that taxpayers' money is well spent, have pushed the need for publicly reported high-stakes tests in literacy and numeracy; this has now become 'the norm' in schools. When systems seek to find out the effectiveness of their schools, curriculum and teaching staff, they might implement a compulsory nation-wide test, often described as a high-stakes test. The results of this type of test provide a data set that can be comparable across groups and/or years, even allowing for learning growth to be measured at national levels.

Yet for school leaders, recent research points clearly to the fact that assessment is an effective practice in classrooms in improving teaching and learning (Black and Wiliam 1998; Snow et al. 1998; Taylor et al. 2005). In contrast to high-stakes tests, assessment might be done at a classroom level or individual child level – and provide an account of what the individual can do or what they need to learn to do.

When assessing literacy, there are 2 ways of looking at this – we can find out what students know by having them write, make, do or say something – while anything else we want to know (or assess) about the learning is obtained by observing them. Logically, asking students to complete a written assessment is an easier and more efficient way of finding out what they know. On the other hand, observing learners takes time and requires skilled observations and a way of comparing these across a sample of learners. In terms of literacy learning, we need an elaborate mix of both of these. In the last 20 to 30 years, we have amassed a significant number of instruments that are commonly used in Australian schools (Forster 2009).

Table 6.1 demonstrates many of the most used assessments, which are presented as those that students complete themselves, or where teachers observe student behaviours. This list is compiled from Forster's (2009) work and discussions with school leaders and teachers.

Table 6.1. Literacy assessments commonly in use in Australia (Forster 2009)

STUDENTS COMPLETE ASSESSMENT	TEACHERS OBSERVE STUDENT BEHAVIOURS
National Assessment Program Literacy and Numeracy (NAPLAN)	Best Start Kindergarten Assessment
PROBE Reading Assessment	Developmental Assessment Resource for Teachers (DART)
Progressive Achievement Tests (PAT-Reading)	First Steps Literacy
Progressive Achievement Tests (Vocabulary Skills)	First Steps: Literacy Indigenous Preschool Profile
Year 2 Diagnostic Net	Informal Prose Inventory (IPI)
Tests of Reading Comprehension (TORCH and TORCH Plus)	Kindergarten and Pre-primary Profile
	Kindergarten Development Check
Progressive Achievement Tests in early years (print, vocabulary, reading comprehension, listening comprehension, phonics)	Performance Indicators in Primary Schools (PIPS) (reading and phonological awareness)
	Running records/Miscue analysis
Burt Word Reading Test	Concepts About Print (CAP)
Neale Analysis of Reading Ability	Observation Survey of Early Literacy Achievement
	National Literacy and Numeracy Learning Progressions
	Dynamic Indicators of Basic Early Literacy Skills (DIBELS)

Table 6.1 indicates that there is a greater range, and perhaps resultant use, of assessment where teachers observe student behaviours than those where students complete assessments themselves. Yet, school effectiveness is currently judged more on the results of assessments that sit in the 'students complete assessment' classification. While there are elements of some of the student-completed tests that can also be used diagnostically, the observational tests can primarily be viewed as a form

of pre-assessment that allows a teacher to determine students' individual strengths, weaknesses, knowledge and skills prior to instruction. These observations or checklists are primarily used to diagnose student difficulties and to guide lesson and curriculum planning.

Table 6.1 shows the prevalence of observation instruments in schools, yet what we don't know is the relationship between the role of observation (the right-hand column) and the shifting results in more traditional tests completed by students (the left-hand column). Common sense tells us that there is a relationship, yet the effect lies in how skilled school and instructional leaders are at using the observation as a basis for intervention. Forster's (2009) work *The evaluation of literacy and numeracy diagnostic tools* was a small scoping study which sought to identify and evaluate the literacy diagnostic tools currently used in Australian school. She tells us that:

> *The central finding of the study is that the 'diagnostic tools' in use in Australian schools vary widely in their conceptualisation and intent, and in the support they provide for teachers. Some tools are developmental frameworks comprising described levels of achievement against which teachers make on-balance judgements on the basis of observations or evidence from instruments of their choice. Some tools are instruments only—vehicles through which evidence of learning is collected and assessed.* (Forster: 2009:2)

Much of this contradiction around collecting evidence of learning based on observations or checklists requires further consideration. The work of Lonigan et al. (2011) begins to draw more specific lines between (i) the nature of the assessment tool, (ii) some examples of the tool, (iii) research reporting ways in which the diagnosis has been shown to be effective and, (iv) a concluding statement that allows insight into the usefulness of the assessment tool and its use by researchers. The following box uses Lonigan et al.'s (2011) categorisations of literacy assessment types and provides evidence-based practices. Lonigan et al. (2011) identify informal assessment, standardised assessment, progress monitoring, screening assessment and diagnostic assessment as the main types of literacy assessment in use. Box 6.1 provides the definition of the assessment type, some examples in common use in Australia, supporting research, and a conclusion about the efficacy and focus of each of the assessment items for school leaders.

Box 6.1. Assessment type and example of classroom and research use

1. **Informal assessment**
   Informal assessment is neither standardised nor highly structured. Usually, this type of assessment simply reflects a teacher's judgement based on casual observation of the child. If there is no comparison metric used it can be difficult to determine whether a child has made or is making adequate progress in skill areas.

   Examples
   - checklists
   - rating scales
   - portfolios of children's work products
   - Best Start Kindergarten Assessment
   - Observation Survey of Early Literacy Achievement
   - Concepts of Print Awareness

   Supporting research
   Beswick et al. (2005) reported a moderate and significant correlation between teachers' ratings of kindergarten students' reading-related skills and a concurrent direct assessment of reading. Whereas other research had very different findings. Graney (2008) found that second-grade teachers were likely to overestimate the rate of growth of children's reading skills. This underscores that assessment needs to be undertaken along with a common-sense focus about achievement.

   Efficacy and focus
   Informal assessments are relatively easy to create and use and can serve as broad screening measures to identify children in need of more rigorous assessments such as diagnostic assessments. Because informal assessments typically do not use a standardised procedure, the conditions of elicitation of children's skills are not uniform across children.

2. **Standardised assessment**

    Standardised measures allow meaningful comparisons among children (or between assessments of a single child over time) because they (a) have clear and consistent administration and scoring criteria (i.e. the measure is always given and scored in the same manner), (b) they demonstrate generally good reliability and validity, and (c) raw scores are converted into scores that reflect a child's performance relative to the performance of a normative group.

    Examples

    > Neale Analysis of Reading Ability – 3rd Edition (tests reading accuracy, comprehension and fluency)
    > Burt Word Reading Test (tests single word recognition)
    > South Australian Spelling Test (tests the ability to write words)
    > Wheldall Assessment of Reading Passages (WARP) (tests reading fluency)
    > MultiLit Word Attack Skills (tests phonic skills)
    > MultiLit Sight Words Placement Tests (tests sight words)

    Supporting research

    A comparative study by Colenbrander et al. (2017) investigated 95 children aged 8 to 12 in Sydney schools. The study found that Neale Analysis of Reading Ability (NARA) comprehension scores were more dependent on decoding skills than York Analysis of Reading Comprehension scores. The Neale Analysis of Reading Ability instructs that once a child has made 16 errors, the test is discontinued. This means that the scores are not suitable for comparisons across class groups as results will not be equal.

    Deacon et al. (2019) used the Burt Word Reading test to establish the value of orthographic knowledge in word learning. Their findings demonstrate that early orthographic learning was related to gains in word reading skills.

    Efficacy and focus

    Standardised assessments provide clear and normed comparisons among different children. The use of these standardised tests continues to provide important base-level data in research studies and in classroom- and school-based interventions. Many of these assessment instruments have been in use for decades and yet continue to attract researcher attention over time (e.g. NARA was first published in 1958 and The Burt Word Reading test in 1981).

3. **Screening assessments**

Screening assessments are typically brief measures that allow a snapshot of children's current skills. These measures are designed so that individuals who have minimal training in assessment can administer them. Results from screening assessments are often interpreted for a child's relative likelihood of needing additional assessment, more careful monitoring, or additional instruction.

A central question concerning the utility of screening assessments is the accuracy – it is reported that there are sometimes false positives (at risk) and false negatives (not at risk). This phenomenon can sometimes make the use of these screening tests in schools problematic.

Examples

> - Kindergarten Development Check
> - Concepts About Print (CAP)
> - Dynamic Indicators of Basic Early Literacy Skills (DIBELS) (tests oral reading fluency)
> - Test of Word Reading Efficiency (TOWRE) (tests word identification fluency)
> - Woodcock-Johnson Diagnostic Reading Battery (tests word identification fluency)

Supporting research

Schaughency et al.'s (2017) research sought to establish if combined contribution of decoding and narrative skills influenced older reading fluency. The use of DIBELS was an important screening instrument for the study as it indicated early reading retelling skills. Thus, its success as an early screening instrument in reading is clear.

Wilson and Lonigan (2010) compared the short-term predictive accuracy of the Get Ready to Read screening tool (GRTR-R) to a diagnostic assessment of early literacy skills in the same sample of preschool children using Indicators of Individual Growth and Development (IGDIs). Whereas both measures performed similarly in identifying true positives (i.e. children with low levels of early literacy skills), the IGDIs produced a higher level of false positives (i.e. children predicted to have low levels of early literacy skills who did not) across outcomes than did the GRTR-R.

Efficacy and focus

Overall, screening measures provide a time-effective, cost-effective and valid means of identifying children with less well-developed early literacy skills However, at present, they do not provide the specific information needed to match instructional support to children's specific needs. Once identified as having low early literacy skills, children will need additional assessment (e.g. diagnostic assessment or other assessment) to determine their specific patterns of strength and weakness to allow effective application of instructional support.

4. **Progress monitoring**

Progress monitoring assessments are brief measures that allow a snapshot of children's skills within a specific area. Progress monitoring assessments allow repeated assessments to determine children's growth in a skill area over time or as a result of instruction.

Progress monitoring assessments are also used to evaluate whether students are responding to instruction and intervention, and to set learning goals or intervention accordingly.

Examples

> National Literacy and Numeracy Learning Progressions

> Performance Indicators in Primary Schools (PIPS) (reading and phonological awareness)

> Progressive Achievement Tests (PAT) Vocabulary Skills

> PAT Early Years Reading

> PAT Reading

> PAT Spelling Skills

Supporting research

A recent analysis of the initial assessment measures in these teacher-administered progress monitoring assessments yielded good evidence of reliability and validity (Goodrich and Lonigan 2010).

Another Australian study by Oakley et al. (2020) used the PIPS (reading and phonological awareness) to investigate whether games and apps on digital devices would improve early reading scores across a large cohort of students in Western Australia. The study found that the reading scores measured by PIPS increased over the period of the intervention.

Efficacy and focus

Progress monitoring assessments can be used as screening assessments (i.e. to determine which children will be monitored frequently or which will receive additional instruction).

Few widely available progress monitoring assessments for early literacy skills are available. Most of these are developed for specific applications, such as for use in a curriculum or for a specific program.

5. **Diagnostic**

   Diagnostic assessments are standardised measures that provide highly detailed information about an individual literacy skill area. Multiple items within the measure are intended to probe and explore different levels of competence or achievement of the skill.

   Diagnostic measures tend to have very prescribed administration procedures. The key advantages of diagnostic assessments include in-depth examination of specific skill areas or facets of a skill area, generally high reliability, established validity of the measure, and the ability to compare a specific child's performance with a known reference group. Hence, these standardised measures allow a meaningful, accurate, and in-depth determination of the early literacy skill areas in which a child has strengths or weaknesses relative to a developmental norm.

   Examples
   - Phonological Awareness Test
   - Peabody Picture Vocabulary Test-4

- Year 2 Diagnostic Net
- Running records
- the Diagnostic Assessment of Reading Comprehension (DARC)
- Woodcock-Johnson Passage Comprehension test
- PAT Early Years Reading
- PAT Reading

Supporting research

Francis et al. (2009) compared 2 diagnostic assessments of reading comprehension — the Woodcock-Johnson Passage Comprehension test, a standard in reading research, and the Diagnostic Assessment of Reading Comprehension (DARC). Their findings show that both diagnostic assessments are influenced by other factors, such as non-verbal reasoning, with the DARC more focused on memory and narrative language production. This shows that diagnostic assessments at times provide very detailed information that may not translate easily in pedagogical practice for all students.

Nichols et al. (2004) found that, along with maturation, a diagnostic approach that guides phonemic awareness instruction and concepts about print enhances kindergarten students' awareness in these areas.

Efficacy and focus

Diagnostic measures are typically lengthy assessments, taking at least 30 minutes to complete. If 30 children were to complete the assessment, that represents at least 15 hours of testing, which is very time consuming for classroom teachers. There should therefore be a focused reason for the use of these tests. Diagnostic tests also have relatively high purchase costs due to the expense of development and often require a degree of specialised training in their administration, scoring and interpretation.

Some diagnostic measures are unable to identify the amount of progress children are making because of exposure to instructional activities.

Intervention

Evidence suggests that diagnostic assessment along with tailored intervention is the best way to improve student literacy achievement. The original concept of tiered intervention came from the United States, following vast federal funding regimes linked to the 'No Child Left Behind' strategy. Reading pedagogy became so politicised after the NRP report (NICHD 2000) that more clarity around resourcing was required. Mesmer and Mesmer (2008) give us a good summary of this Response to Intervention (RTI) movement:

> *Despite the challenges with Response to Intervention (RTI), we have seen this approach increase the quantity and quality of instruction for struggling readers. RTI is an initial attempt to provide an alternative model to the dominant and damaging discrepancy model in which so much time is spent admiring the student's reading problem. By this we mean that people discuss the problem, collect data on it, and write about it, months before they do anything about it. (Mesmer and Mesmer 2008: 289).*

A number of influential researchers have conducted empirical studies to explore the best ways forward in relation to early intervention. For example, Coyne et al. (2004) explored the metaphors of 'inoculation and insulin' in kindergarten classrooms – inoculation referring to early reading intervention around sound-symbol relationships and insulin referring to the need for ongoing support to maintain early positive effects of intervention. Coyne et al.'s (2004) study found that the positive effects of intervention in Kindergarten did provide a strong base for reading as the students in the study progressed from Kindergarten to Year 1.

However, most importantly from this study there is a cautionary statement from Coyne's (2001) earlier work – 'Moreover, schools are complex host environments, and the complicated interactions that occur between teachers, curricula, and policies within a school make it very difficult to coordinate intervention efforts, (Coyne 2001).' This serves as an introduction to Figure 6.1.

Intervention and supporting literacy learners

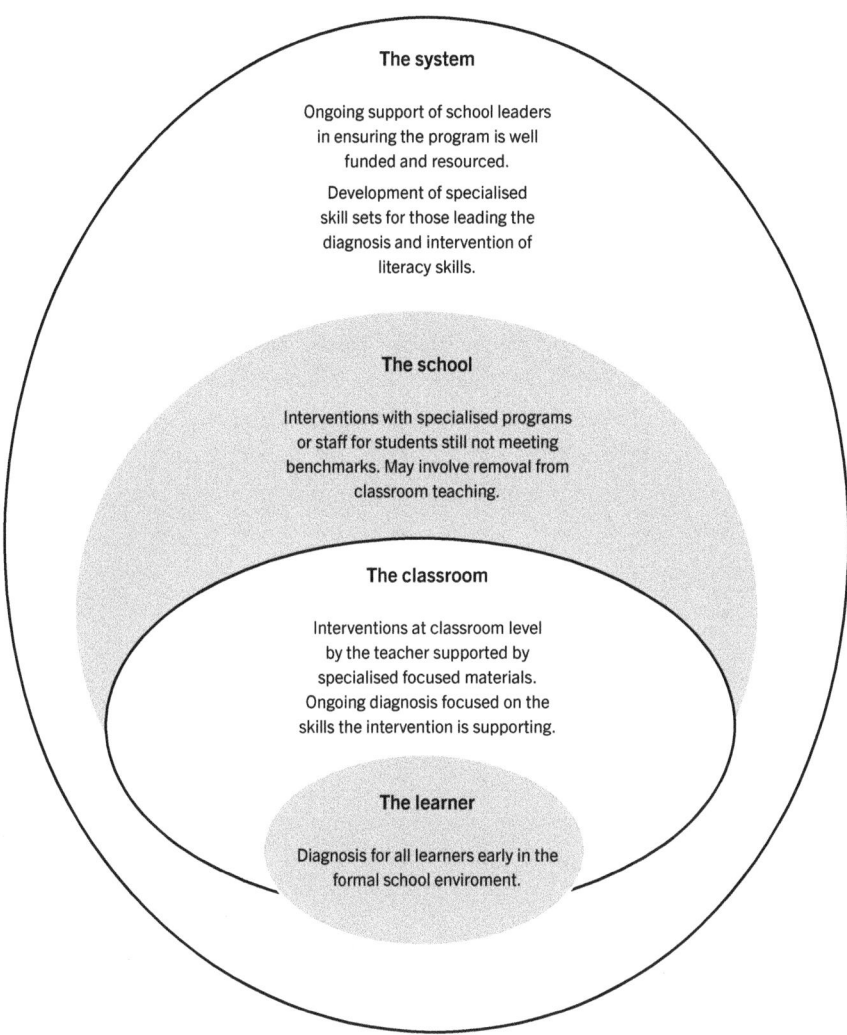

Figure 6.1. Schools, systems and learners – a community of intervention

Strategies to help literacy achievement in your school

When assessing and collecting data about students' strengths and areas for development, school leaders need to be familiar with the tests and assessment tools available. The next step is to decide the level of detail that is required from the assessment and Lonigan et al.'s (2011) work makes this clearer. What type of assessment yields what type of data, and for what purpose? Finally, using measurement instruments that focus on a number of skills concurrently, or an assessment task that requires the learner to orchestrate a large number of literacy skills at the same time will deliver a 'blunt' finding (for example, the NAPLAN reading tests), whereas some learners might be better served by an instrument that focuses on one or 2 skills (for example, miscue analysis). ACER has developed a large body of materials and assessment instruments over many years that provide a range of assessments. Several of these provide progress monitoring, a standardised assessment process, and diagnostic abilities. These materials are well known to school leaders and teachers who have utilised the Progressive Achievement Test (PAT) range of tests to diagnose, group and monitor pupils for some time. Table 6.2 details some of the Progressive Achievement Tests available and in use in schools across Australia and, increasingly, in other countries.

Table 6.2. ACER Progressive Achievement Tests for literacy

PROGRESSIVE ACHIEVEMENT TESTS	DESCRIPTION
PAT Reading	Assesses reading comprehension and measures growth from Years 1 to 10.
PAT Early Years Reading	Four assessments targeting emergent reading skills (e.g. decoding) and comprehension in the first 2 years of schooling, supporting early intervention.
PAT Spelling Skills	Assesses the skills underpinning spelling for a comprehensive understanding of spelling knowledge and ability.
PAT Spelling	Assesses knowledge of spelling and skills in identifying and correcting spelling errors.
PAT Grammar and Punctuation	Assesses understanding of the standard Australian English language conventions of grammar and punctuation.
PAT Vocabulary Skills	Measures the breadth and depth of vocabulary and associated processing skills for a comprehensive understanding of vocabulary knowledge and ability.
PAT Vocabulary	Assesses word knowledge through synonyms.

More recently, ACER have developed the PAT Reading Adaptive test. This measures reading literacy and comprehension with the test content personalised to each student, allowing school leaders to gain more meaningful data for planning and school leadership purposes.

Another example of assessment and diagnostic tests is First Steps (Department of Education Western Australia 2013), which provides a map of observable behaviour in the 4 main areas of language (listening, speaking, reading and writing). Uniquely, it also provides help for teachers to make informed, strategic decisions about how to support students' literacy development. First Steps materials were reviewed by the Department of Education Western Australia in 2013 and provide the link between observation and planning for teaching and learning that many similar observation instruments lack.

As mentioned earlier, evidence further suggests that diagnostic assessment together with tailored intervention is the best way to take that step to raise student achievement in literacy, provided the assessment is carefully chosen and the school leadership is committed and able to bring the staff along. A useful definition of teacher leadership from the literature is that

> *leadership facilitates principled action to achieve whole-school success. It applies the distinctive power of teaching to shape meaning for children, youth and adults. And it contributes to long-term, enhanced quality of community life. (Crowther et al. 2009: xvii)*

In Australia, teacher leadership and school improvement planning are supported in each jurisdiction with targeted funding and intervention models. The interaction between targeted literacy funding and tiered intervention rests with the school leader. The responsibility is huge and complex, and tiered intervention can help address this. Schools often work within a multi-tier Response to Intervention framework based on the data collected through assessment, diagnosis and analysis. Vaughn and Fuchs (2003) underscore this process when they suggest that general education and special education teachers work together to systematically assess problems and intervene as part of the general education cycle. Many jurisdictions in Australia have very sophisticated models for instructional support for these interventions, with funding from systems tied to diagnosis and intervention in literacy and numeracy. At times, there are staff allocations linked to these interventions and changes to general education provision. Figure 6.2 illustrates the Australian interpretation of the Response to Intervention.

Tier 1: Classroom instruction
- This is whole-school and classroom-based interventions. It involves teachers having professional development opportunities to learn how to gather evidence and diagnose class learning needs around reading. It includes the support of school leaders and, at times, instructional leadership, such as that offered by literacy coaches. Classroom instruction supports identification of students who need further intervention.

Tier 2: Small group classroom instruction
- This is where students identified as needing support are supported in classrooms by the instructional leader and at all times by the classroom teacher. The classroom teacher is informed by the diagnosis and provided with leadership from the instructional leader. Often, support offered by the instructional leader is done in small groups of students with similar needs.

Tier 3: Individual instruction
- This is where individual learners are given intensive interventions aimed to support them to access the curriculum. These are evidence-based interventions that might be tailored to the individual or small group and are conducted outside the classroom by the improvement teacher.

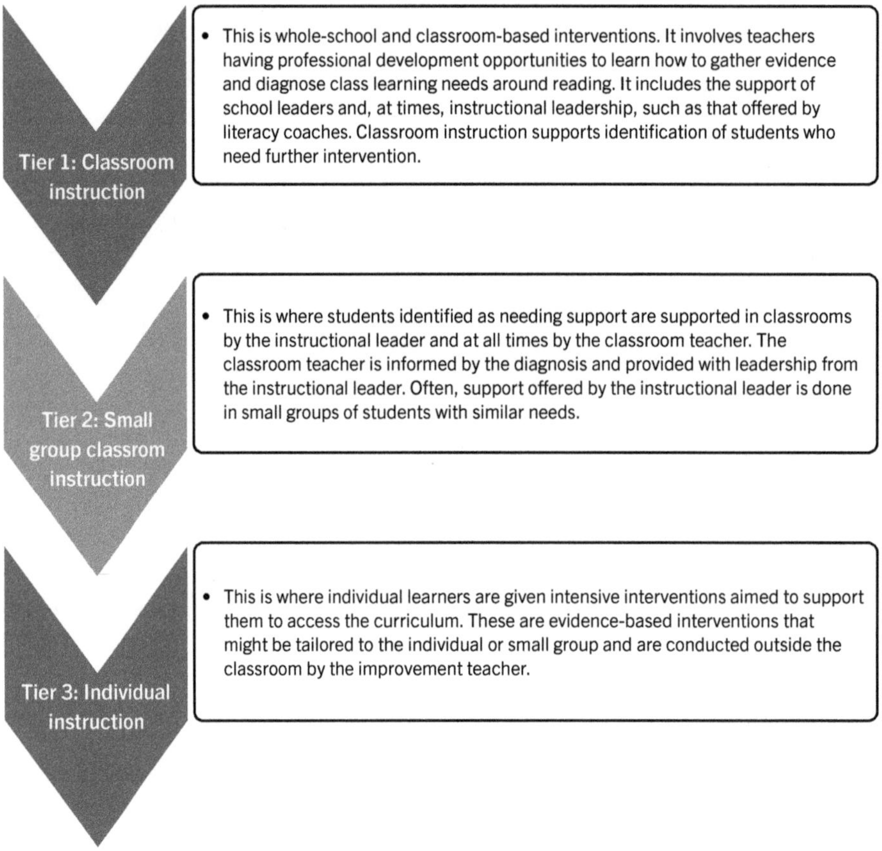

Figure 6.2. Australian interpretation of the Response to Intervention (RTI)

To support struggling readers in the classroom, including those with learning disabilities, the best designed interventions possible should be available. It has been long established that we need interventions with strong effects for improved literacy and improved long-term outcomes. RTI reminds us that intervention based on early evidence is a far more sensible way forward than responding to literacy problems later in the school years. Research into the implementation of RTI offers us evidence that this is effective. For example, the research by Graves et al. (2011) indicates that Tier 2 instruction, combined with evidence-based Tier 1 interventions, has a significant impact on Grade 6 students with and without learning disabilities.

In Australia, the writing of Hempenstall (2012) underscores the 'game changing' impact of RTI when she says:

> *Response to Intervention shifts our attention from the characteristics of the learner to those of the teaching process. As educators, our capacity to influence student performance is more fruitfully focused upon what we can contribute rather than solely on what the student brings. The environment and what conditions promote achievement become our tools. A consequence of this change is that we no longer require struggling students to obtain some form of diagnosis before we act. We can observe and act immediately.* (Hempenstall 2012: 130)

Schools are well placed to implement operational change to meet the needs of learners in a timely manner.

Reflections from school leaders

This is written by Imogene Cochrane Bond, a deputy principal in an inner-city school who has grappled with a school-based intervention model and shares her thoughts below.

Question 1: What does a school-based approach to diagnosis and remediation in literacy programs look like?

Building a complete and nuanced picture of student achievement in literacy across a school is integral to the work of teachers and school leaders and essential for maintaining high levels of student growth.

It is important that school leaders work collaboratively to coordinate the use of a broad range of diagnostic tools in order to discern where individuals are at in their literacy development and then plan for and resource a program of tiered intervention as appropriate.

Diagnostic tools can be both formal and informal, with an emphasis on those that are accessible for teachers, simple to embed in classroom practice and will collect data in a timely fashion. These could include gathering data through the use of reading running records, externally developed assessments of comprehension and vocabulary, such as the Progressive Achievement Tests (PAT) or the York Assessment of Reading Comprehension (YARC), assessments of skills in phonics and phonemic awareness, teacher observations during structured guided reading sessions, moderated student writing samples and evidence of oral language use in the classroom.

School leaders should support their teaching teams in the early identification of individuals requiring remediation and then ideally work across teams to identify patterns of need across the school in order to best distribute and coordinate resources. Literacy remediation across the school prioritises early intervention and offers a tiered and targeted approach. Small numbers of students may be offered intensive, individualised support from a specialist practitioner, while others may be offered small group interventions delivered by support staff within the classroom context. Other students may be given specific learning goals accompanied by explicit instruction from the teacher to move them forward. A teacher's literacy program should always reflect their understanding of the specific literacy needs of the students in their classroom and be tailored accordingly. Teachers also need to be supported to coordinate with any external providers of specialist interventions.

Where school leaders have identified common areas of need across year groups or in some cases the whole school, any remediation program should be accompanied by a rigorous plan for teacher professional learning that will ensure classroom teachers are well equipped to deliver high-quality classroom teaching and learning experiences to address these areas of need.

Question 2: Do you think a whole-school focus on diagnosis and remediation in literacy contributes to raising student achievement?

Student achievement is certainly maximised in settings where teachers, school leaders, parents and external specialists in the community work collaboratively to achieve measurable student growth.

A whole-school, systematic focus on diagnosis ensures that students encountering difficulties are identified as early as possible and that the underlying reasons for these difficulties are clear. Generally, budgetary resources available for schools to put towards literacy remediation and intervention are limited and so whole-school coordination of these resources ensures that early intervention is targeted to the individual students who need it the most and that other tiered interventions can be directed to impact the largest possible number of students.

While student remediation and growth in literacy is always a focus, so too is ensuring measurable growth in teachers' knowledge and pedagogical skills to teach literacy effectively. When school leadership works to synchronise student remediation in literacy with teacher professional development, student achievement can be raised and the need for intensive levels of intervention can be reduced over the long term.

School-wide improvement

Mesmer and Mesmer (2008: 238) provide a strong summary for school intervention communities with an action plan. Many school systems are doing just this and often this falls to the instructional leader who may be appointed to a school to embed the Response to Intervention (RTI) model. I have reproduced the key steps in this process in Figure 6.3 as it may provide some direction for school leaders and serve as a possible blueprint for practice.

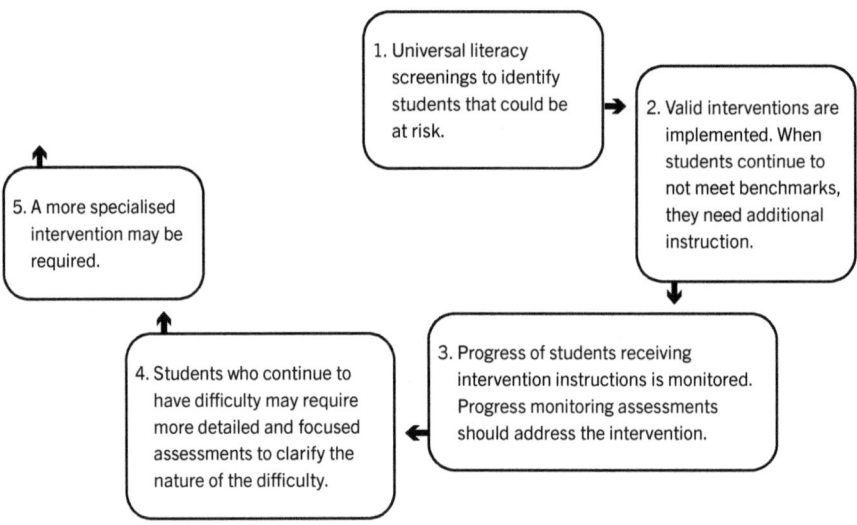

Figure 6.3. An intervention pattern (based on Mesmer and Mesmer 2008)

The diagnosis and intervention will be successful when each child learning to read and write is given the opportunity to be supported through the 5 steps shown in Figure 6.3. Schools are seemingly very good at identifying students that are progressing well and those who might be at risk, at building data walls and at discussing the needs of those learners identified as requiring intervention. However, we need to remain watchful that these students' progress is monitored carefully and that the next steps for intervention are considered and ready. We should all keep in mind Mesmer and Mesmer's (2008: 289) warning about 'admiring the student's reading problem' rather than doing something about it.

A study by Spear-Swerling and Cheesman (2012) surveyed 142 US-based elementary teachers regarding their classroom preparedness for carrying out the Response to Intervention (RTI) model described previously, as well as aspects of reading and assessment. The percentages of correct answers to the questions in the survey ranged from about 58 to 65 per cent. Most participants were familiar with basic features of RTI, such as the 3-tiered model but were unfamiliar with the research-based instructional approaches and interventions named in the study questionnaire. This suggests that participants who had experienced close reading instruction and training in conducting diagnostic observation tools, such as miscue analysis, were significantly more likely to be familiar with certain interventions. The study also suggests that professional development is important to enable educators to implement RTI effectively in reading. Many schools in Australia have the valuable resource of reading recovery teachers who have been redeployed into classrooms or instructional leader positions and are waiting to support others in the literacy teaching community of practice (Lave and Wenger 1991).

REFERENCES

Alderson C (2005) *Diagnosing foreign language proficiency. The interface between learning and assessment*, Continuum, London.

Beswick JF, Willms D and Sloat EA (2005) 'A comparative study of teacher ratings of emergent literacy skills and student performance on a standardized measure', *Education*, 126:116–137.

Black P and Wiliam D (1998) 'Inside the black box: raising standards through classroom assessment,' *Phi Delta Kappan*, 80(2):139–47.

Childs-Bowen D, Moller G and Scrivner J (2000) 'Principals: leaders of leaders', *NASSP bulletin*, 84(616):27–34.

Colenbrander D, Nickels L and Kohnen S (2017) 'Similar but different: differences in comprehension diagnosis on the Neale Analysis of Reading Ability and the York Assessment of Reading for Comprehension', *Journal of Research in Reading*, 40:403–419.

Cox, R (2015a) '"What language are you?": A glimpse into multilingual childhoods', *English in Australia*, 50(1):49–54.

Cox, R (2015b) 'Contextualising multilingualism in Australia today', *English in Australia*, 50(1):13–20.

Coyne MD (2001) *Kindergarten reading intervention: inoculation or insulin?* [unpublished doctoral dissertation], University of Oregon, Eugene.

Coyne MD, Kame'enui EJ, Simmons DC and Harn BA (2004) Beginning reading intervention as inoculation or insulin: first-grade reading performance of strong responders to kindergarten intervention, *Journal of Learning Disabilities*, 37(2):90–104.

Crowther F, Ferguson M and Hann L (2009) *Developing teacher leaders: how teacher leadership enhances school success*, Corwin Press, Thousand Oaks, CA.

Deacon SH, Pasquarella A, Marinus E, Tims T and Castles A (2019) 'Orthographic processing and children's word reading', *Applied Psycholinguistics*, 40(2):509–534.

Department of Education WA (2013) *First steps literacy*, Department of Education Western Australia website, accessed 16 March 2022. http://det.wa.edu.au/stepsresources/detcms/navigation/first-steps-literacy/

Durrant C and Cox R (2015) 'English teaching in globalised educational contexts', *English in Australia*, 50(1):2–7.

Forster M (2009) *Literacy and numeracy diagnostic tools: an evaluation*, Department of Education, Employment and Workplace Relations (DEEWR), Canberra.

Francis D, Snow CE, August D, Carlson CD, Miller J and Iglesias A (2009) 'Measures of reading comprehension: a latent variable analysis of diagnostic assessment of reading comprehension', *Scientific Studies in Reading*, 10(3):301–322.

Goodrich JM and Lonigan CJ (2010) *Accuracy of teacher-administered assessments of preschool children's early language and literacy skills*, paper presented at the Fifth Annual Institute of Education Sciences Research Conference, Washington, DC.

Graney SB (2008) General education teacher judgments of their low-performing students' short-term reading progress, *Psychology in the Schools*, 45:537–549.

Graves AW, Brandon R, Duesbery L, McIntosh A, and Pyle NB (2011) 'The effects of tier 2 literacy instruction in sixth grade: toward the development of a response-to-intervention model in middle school', *Learning Disability Quarterly*, 34(1):73–86.

Hempenstall K (2012) 'Response to intervention: accountability in action', *Australian Journal of Learning Difficulties*, 17(2):101–131.

Lave J and Wenger E (1991) *Situated learning: legitimate peripheral participation*, Cambridge University Press, Cambridge.

Lonigan CJ, Allan NP and Lerner MD (2011) 'Assessment of preschool early literacy skills: linking children's educational needs with empirically supported instructional activities', *Psychology in the Schools*, 48(5):488–501.

Mesmer EM and Mesmer HE (2008) 'Response to Intervention (RTI): what teachers of reading need to know,' The Reading Teacher 62(4):280-290.

NICHD (National Institute of Child Health and Human Development) (2000) *Report of the National Reading Panel: teaching children to read: reports of the subgroups*. National Institute of Child Health and Human Development, National Institutes of Health, Washington, DC.

Nichols WD, Rupley WH, Rickelman RJ and Algozzine B (2004) 'Examining phonemic awareness and concepts of print patterns of kindergarten students', *Reading Research and Instruction,* 43(3):56–82.

Oakley G, Wildy H and Berman YE (2020) 'Multimodal digital text creation using tablets and open-ended creative apps to improve the literacy learning of children in early childhood classrooms', *Journal of Early Childhood Literacy*, 20(4):655–679.

Ogawa RT and Bossert ST (1995) 'Leadership as an organizational quality', *Educational Administration Quarterly*, 31:224–243.

Schaughency E, Suggate S and Reese E (2017) 'Links between early oral narrative and decoding skills and later reading in a New Zealand sample', *Australian Journal of Learning Difficulties*, 22(2):109–132.

Snow CE, Burns MS and Griffin P (1998) *Preventing reading difficulties in young children*, National Academy Press, Washington, DC.

Spear-Swerling L and Cheesman E (2012) 'Teachers' knowledge base for implementing response-to-intervention models in reading' *Read Writing*, 25:1691–1723.

Taylor BM, Pearson PD, Peterson D and Rodriguez MC (2005) 'The CIERA school change framework: an evidence-based approach to professional development and school reading improvement', *Reading Research Quarterly*, 40(1):40–69.

Vaughn S and Fuchs LS (2003) 'Redefining learning disabilities as inadequate response to instruction: the promise and potential problems,' *Learning Disabilities: Research & Practice*, 18:137–146.

Wilson SB and Lonigan CJ (2009) 'Emergent literacy screeners for preschool children: an evaluation of Get Ready to Read! and individual growth and development indicators', *Annals of Dyslexia*, 59:115–131.

CHAPTER 7

Conclusion

This book has presented high-impact practices in teaching literacy by focusing on key elements that research has shown are successful in supporting and improving achievement in literacy in your school.

Chapter 1 introduced evidence-based teaching and the resultant labelling of practices that have high impact, as well as defining key terms and processes underpinning educational research. It provides some critical knowledge and checkpoints for navigating the complex terrain of educational research and shows how classroom practice, and the decisions made by school leaders in relation to the decisions of system leaders, might be aligned with research evidence.

Chapter 2 continued in this vein by introducing research evidence that points to the importance of oral language in the development of early literacy skills and in the growth of reading skills beyond the foundation years. This discussion of oral language also provides a rich research base and strategies around classroom talk and maximising talk for LOTE students and highlights the significance of adopting specific oral language programs at a school system or policy level.

In Chapter 3, we looked at research that shows that grammar delivered in isolation may not improve outcomes, but that when it is taught in the context of writing, meaningful connections can be made. Research that identified a lack of teacher knowledge of grammar was also discussed. Useful tools for the explicit teaching of grammar include Myhill and colleagues' 'playful explicitness' model, which encompasses experimentation, developing a shared language around language choices, using grammatical metalanguage, utilising mentor texts and supporting students as designers of writing. A knowledge of grammar, and with that a shared metalanguage, should be central to reading and viewing, writing and representing, and listening and speaking throughout the school day and a learner's school experiences. A shared grammar is also important at a school-wide level.

We moved on to consider vocabulary in Chapter 4 – one of the National Reading Panel report's (NICHD 2000) 'big five' reading practices. While earlier work tended to focus on teaching vocabulary in 'isolation', recent research has placed more emphasis on teaching vocabulary within the context of 'the meaning aspects' (morphology) of language structure. Among other work, we considered Snow et al.'s (2009) Word Generation program and explored the 3-tiered model for selecting vocabulary commonly employed in schools. Another useful tool from this section is the model for teaching vocabulary provided in Figure 4.1. It draws on existing research and focuses on 5 core elements – select word choice, repeated and rich exposure, encouragement of vocabulary use and experimentation, provision of word learning strategies, and teaching spelling and vocabulary together (employing word lists linked through common spelling and meaning).

In Chapter 5, we focused on the teaching of reading. The National Reading Panel report (NICHD 2000) found that the 'big five' – phonemic awareness, phonics instruction, fluency, vocabulary knowledge and reading comprehension – all contributed to reading improvement. To these, we can add the sixth dimension of oral language, which Konza and colleagues have argued is also significant in supporting the learning of reading. But these elements are not all equally important nor do they all occur simultaneously, as noted in Paris's argument that some skills are constrained to earlier years of learning and others are learnt continually. Another widely adopted and evidenced-based approach to teaching reading evolved from the work of Fountas and Pinell and includes the strategies of guided reading, literature discussion, interactive read-aloud, independent reading with conferences and reading minilessons. Although Fountas and Pinnell's work is grounded on levelled-readers, they argue against the overuse of these tools and against 'labelling' students using levels. Tools like levelled and decoded readers are useful for teachers but reading programs can also be enriched through maintaining a rich array of reading resources, including 'real books'. Duke and Pearson's (2009) summary of evidence-based reading comprehension strategies also provides valuable direction, encompassing prediction, teacher and student think-aloud, text structure, visual representation, questioning and summarisation. A final model that school leaders and teachers can take away from this chapter is that of Axford et al. (2009), which recommends a process of discerning text selection by the teacher, followed by steps orienting students to text, aural content and language that in turn lead to fluent scaffolded reading. This is beneficial, in particular, for students for whom English is not a first language and who might benefit from more explicit scaffolding.

Finally, Chapter 6 gave us an overview of assessment and intervention programs in place in schools, reviewing those that have the strongest evidence base, are in common use, and have been found to be useful. Diagnostic tools, in particular, enable in-depth examination of specific skill areas and offer high reliability. We also considered the significance of the Response to Intervention model that emerged in the US, which reminds us that intervention based on early evidence is more effective than responding later in the school years. It is important that assessments are chosen carefully, and the effectiveness of assessments also lies in how they are used as a basis for intervention. In the world of diagnosis and intervention in literacy, 'all that glitters is not always gold'. Two useful diagnostic assessments highlighted in our discussion include the Australian Council for Educational Research's Progressive Achievement Tests (PAT) and First Steps developed in Western Australia. We also describe the 3-tired model of intervention used in Australia and indicate that combining the different types of instruction and intervention in the model can contribute to improvement in literacy achievement.

In their Response to Intervention discussion, Mesmer and Mesmer (2008) also repeat a warning made by Pressley (2003) – that scientific research or experiments as the best way to intervene with learners in the teaching of reading is often problematic to implement because the support offered during the experiment is not there for everyday classroom events. They go further to sound a warning to schools and school leaders when they say,

> *if scientifically based interventions are to be implemented, then research findings must get to schools. We are concerned that the label* scientifically based *will be misused and will proliferate as publishers and companies slap it on everything they market to schools.* (Mesmer and Mesmer 2008: 289)

In summarising the 5 high-impact literacy practices discussed in this book, some common threads become evident. One of these is that each of the elements rarely work best when taught in isolation. Instead, better outcomes are often more likely when areas of literacy teaching are integrated and linked more directly with tasks. In our discussions in each chapter around school-wide improvement and in the insightful school leader reflections included throughout the book, some other core themes have emerged. It is important that there are shared visions, goals, language and responsibilities around literacy programs in schools. The Australian Curriculum: English and other syllabi, as well as results from some external measures and internal assessments, can be useful starting points in navigating literacy programs. But school leaders should also promote open discussion around literacy and ensure that professional learning and support is a part of a whole-school approach. School leaders need to be confident in teachers, their instructional leadership and, most importantly, their system leadership. Schools have a wealth of skill and knowledge and, oftentimes, resources just waiting for a capable leader to lead.

While Chapter 6 touched on specialised intervention programs, it should be acknowledged at this point that our discussion has largely considered approaches for mainstream students, or rather, most students in the learning context. School leaders and teachers know, however, that in every group of learners there is a vast range of diversity. In literacy education, there is a diversity of language background, whether a child might be a monolingual English speaker, a bilingual English speaker, a multilingual English speaker or a speaker of another dialect of English. My own recent work (Cox 2015a, 2015b) explores multilingualism in Australia today by referring to immigration trends and globalisation and looking at research into the language use and choices of multilingual primary-aged children in Sydney schools. Further to this, my work with Durrant (Durrant and Cox 2015) discusses some elements of First Nations language use in Australia, using an historical lens.

Schools must adjust and deliver curriculum in literacy that meets the learning needs of all children. Some schools have greater linguistic and cultural diversity than others and some have a more homogenous population. All schools also have a vast range of abilities, and this often emerges during initial literacy experiences. It is beyond the scope of this book to cover all elements of these diverse learning needs.

As a final point, I would like to return to that day in country NSW when I heard Fiona Stanley talk about 'causal pathways' on the radio. As we have demonstrated in this book, we do have a rich set of research studies that point us in the general direction of knowing what our causal pathways are in literacy education. We have robust evidence and many years of this (see the National Reading Panel [NICHD 2000] evidence chapters), but there is a marked difference in the context of Dr Stanley's work. Our research evidence comes from the behaviour and messy, tangled worlds of schools and children's words. We have to use other insights to help work out these causal pathways in schools – these are our professional judgement and knowledge of our school context and communities. This is what school leaders have in spades. Increasingly, within this complex terrain, teachers and school leaders are required to understand the work of educational researchers and 'what counts as evidence'. School leaders must also be acknowledged for the professional knowledge and skills that enable them to navigate the complexities of educational systems every day, while they also strive to ensure the best educational outcomes for each student.

REFERENCES

Axford B, Harders P and Wise F (2009) *Scaffolding literacy: an integrated and sequential approach to teaching reading, spelling and writing*, ACER Press, Camberwell, VIC.

Cox, R (2015a) '"What language are you?": A glimpse into multilingual childhoods', *English in Australia*, 50(1):49-54.

Cox, R (2015b) 'Contextualising multilingualism in Australia today', *English in Australia*, 50(1):13-20.

Durrant C and Cox R (2015) 'English teaching in globalised educational contexts', *English in Australia*, 50(1):2-7.

Mesmer EM and Mesmer HE (2008) 'Response to Intervention (RTI): what teachers of reading need to know,' The Reading Teacher 62(4):280-290.

NICHD (National Institute of Child Health and Human Development) (2000) *Report of the National Reading Panel: teaching children to read: reports of the subgroups*. National Institute of Child Health and Human Development, National Institutes of Health, Washington, DC.

www.ingramcontent.com/pod-product-compliance
Lightning Source LLC
Chambersburg PA
CBHW061126070526
44584CB00033B/4228